BI 3079454 4

KU-490-345

# An Early Start to Drama

## Jenny Griffiths

SIMON & SCHUSTER
EDUCATION

**Text** © Jenny Griffiths 1991
**Design and artwork** © Simon & Schuster Education 1991
**Photographs** © The sources credited

All rights reserved

First published in 1991 in Great Britain by
Simon & Schuster Education
Wolsey House, Wolsey Road
Hemel Hempstead, Herts HP2 4SS

Printed in Great Britain by
BPCC Hazell Books, Paulton and Aylesbury

British Library Cataloguing in Publication Data
Griffiths, Jenny
    An early start to drama
    1. Drama
    I. Title
    808.2

ISBN 0 7501 0119 9

**Series editor:** John Day
**Editor:** Annie Scothern
**Design and artwork:** Julia Osorno
**Cover artwork:** Shirley Tourret

**Photo credits**
Hulton-Deutsch Collection (page 58)
Illustrated London News Picture Library (page 59)
Imperial War Museum (page 71)
Popperfoto (page 77)
Raphael Tuck and Sons (page 70)

The author and publishers thank the above for permission to
reproduce their photographs.

**Other acknowledgements**
The author and publishers thank Noel Gay Music Co. Ltd.
for their permission to reproduce on page 75 the chorus from
*Run, Rabbit – Run!*

The extracts on page 77 are taken from the following publications:
Jackson, C., *Who Will Take Our Children?*, Methuen, 1985
Westall, R., *Children of the Blitz*, Viking, 1985
Haining, P., *The Day War Broke Out*, W.H. Allen and Co., 1989
Croall, J., *Don't You Know There's a War On?*, Hutchinson, 1988
*Where's Your Horns?*, Spitalfields Books, 1979
Westall, R., *Children of the Blitz*, Viking, 1985
Ward, S., *War in the Countryside*, Cameron Books, 1988

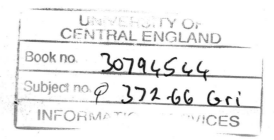
UNIVERSITY OF
CENTRAL ENGLAND
Book no. 30794544
Subject no. 372.66 Gri
INFORMATIC SERVICES

## Drama as a learning medium

The idea of attempting some drama fills many teachers with trepidation, producing comments such as: 'It's something I know nothing about', 'I'm not an actor', 'I don't know where to begin', 'It's bound to be chaotic', but try and sweep all those preconceived ideas away for a moment. Many of them are linked to the 'performance' aspect of drama, which is not what this book is about. Here we are looking at drama as a learning medium, something through which you teach, in the same way you do through using books, the computer, the blackboard, art and craft materials and so on. It is a way of learning and, having its origins in play, capitalises on the child's enthusiasm for this familiar and much-loved method of discovery. In the classroom, however, drama is not simply play, transposed untouched from the playground; the activity is structured so that the participants are encouraged to explore new and unknown areas. Often, initial responses need to be challenged or refined in the face of further thought, and here the teacher has a vital role to play. Just as you would not expect your class to negotiate its way through maths or science without your intervention, so in drama you are needed, to encourage, question, focus attention, listen, query, pose problems, spark off new trains of thought, play devil's advocate, bolster confidence and in many other ways open up the area under investigation. You may say that teachers are endeavouring to do these things throughout their teaching anyway, so why should they bother with drama? I would reply that, besides adding variety to your teaching, drama is a very immediate and exciting medium to work in. The way you relate to your class through drama activities 'feels' different to you and to them, giving rise to new insights both about the material you are working on and about each other.

Drama is unusual in that it is both a subject in its own right and also a 'teaching tool' that can be used to explore other subjects. It is in the latter mode that it is employed in this book. Its ideas and ways of working can be adapted to any area you wish to explore with your class and need not be confined to those set out in the topics offered here. You do not need specialist knowledge, but you do need to be prepared to approach the work seriously and in partnership with your class; it is something you are going to work on and create together. The teacher using drama as a learning medium does not approach the class with a body of knowledge that he or she intends to impart *to* them but rather recognises, and allows the class to recognise, that both he or she and they have discoveries to make and that all contributions, if made with commitment, are equally valid.

At the risk of stating the obvious, it is worth remembering that you cannot do drama without having something to do drama about, and material can be found right across the curriculum. Just a glance through the topics in this book will show how using drama to create 'as if' situations produces a multitude of needs that have to be met, and in meeting them the participants find themselves using and extending their mathematical, scientific, linguistic, historical or geographical skills and understanding. This same process also presents activities and problems that make demands on the child's personal and social capabilities by addressing personal attitudes, social responsibilities and moral ideas and behaviour.

The book is organised in a way that presumes that work in drama will be set within a context of other activities on a particular subject. The amount of drama you use is for you to decide; it can be as much or as little as you wish. Although, for the sake of clarity, the ideas for each topic are set out with a beginning, a middle and an end, you do not have to follow that order or indeed use everything that is there. You may wish the medium of drama to be your main way of approaching the topic, in which case you might use much of the material in that section. On the other hand, if you are dealing with a topic largely through other media, you may only want to use one drama idea. You could, for example, take the myth-telling sequence in *Famine* or the three-tableaux strategy from *Castles and Village Life* or the meeting with Mrs Besant in *Matchgirls* and use drama on that one aspect of the topic only, approaching the rest through other methods.

You will notice that most of the work emphasises the process and not the product, and I think it is fairly clear that this form of drama is about learning from 'doing' rather than about 'showing'. There are one or two ideas for sharing the experiences of the class with others, but I would stress that any presentation should grow out of the group's work and be a recognisably organic part of it, rather than something that is tagged on at the end or superimposed on a body of work to which it bears little relation.

There are occasions in the text when you will find demonstrations of potential verbal responses. They are there purely to give you an idea of what to expect, and under no circumstances should the participants be given those words to say, as in a play. The whole point of using drama as a learning medium is that the children are asked to think independently, to generate and shape their own ideas and find appropriate language with which to express themselves.

## Organisation and control

### Grouping

The four basic ways of organising the class to work in drama are exactly the same as those you would use in the rest of your teaching: individual, pair, group, or whole class work. There are different advantages attached to each way of working and ideally you would aim to employ some of each type, if not in each session, then certainly over the course of several sessions. It is important that variety is incorporated both in the organisation and in the strategies you use. We all feel safe with the familiar and wary of the new, and if a class gets used to working in only one or two ways the children are likely to look askance at any later changes you may want to introduce. Paradoxically they may, at the same time, become bored with the familiar ways and lose interest, so it is doubly important that work does not become predictable, and the children are not able to forecast exactly what they will be doing at every drama session.

### Spaces

Drama does not necessarily have to take place in a hall or other large space. In fact, such places can sometimes be counterproductive if the drama to be undertaken is of a small-scale, sensitive or thoughtful nature. The hall can also be equated in the children's minds with vigorous physical activity, as in PE, and you may judge that starting off in the classroom would produce a more appropriate atmosphere. You will see that many of the activities suggested in the topics lend themselves very readily to classroom spaces. If, however, you are working in a large area, do consider whether it would be helpful to restrict or define the spaces to be used. This can be done in many ways. For example, there are several good reasons why the classic circle which opens many drama lessons is used so frequently: everyone has equal status, everyone's face can be seen, a contained space is created in the centre which can be used to work in, and the fact that drama is a cooperative task with everyone working together is emphasised. If groups are working separately, they will be helped to focus by establishing their own private spaces that are recognised by all.

### Objects – real or imagined?

As a rule-of-thumb it is usually helpful *not* to use classroom objects as substitutes for real ones, such as rulers for swords or bags for babies. It is very easy to get yourself in the position I once found myself in when the contents of what seemed like every container in the classroom were piled up as the belongings of a community on the move! It took a long time to get it all sorted out again and put back in its proper place. It is often much better to use imagination to furnish a space; a group pushing an imaginary loaded cart is likely to have a more believable experience than one that is attempting to move a precariously built pile of chairs. Having said that, there may be occasions when you feel it would be helpful to use real, as opposed to imagined, objects and if that is the case then try to use substantial articles, ones that feel and look right.

### Stopping to take stock

Another point to bear in mind is that the drama can be stopped at any time for discussion, clarification, or if decisions need to be taken which cannot be dealt with in-role from within the drama. There is no sense in which drama, once begun, is a roller-coaster that cannot be stopped. If you feel worried about losing control, for example, then stop, look with the children at the problem that is threatening to destroy the work, deal with it and then, if it is appropriate, pick up the drama again and go on. It is important for your class to recognise that while drama should be enjoyable and is often fun, it is still work, and the children have a responsibility to approach what they do with commitment both to it and to each other; that it is, in fact, this working together that makes the drama happen.

### Ways of stopping

It is useful to establish your way or ways of stopping activities once they are in full swing. Some people like to call out the word 'Freeze', which does suggest that action is not necessarily coming to a full stop but is being held

in suspended animation and can be picked up again straight away. Others prefer to use something like a tambour which, sensitively used, can produce a variety of sounds that may be appropriate at different times. Still others like to establish a chair or area to which they go when they want the class to stop and gather round to listen. Most teachers probably use a combination of these and obviously everyone eventually evolves his or her own, but it is important to give thought to how you are going to stop *before* you begin! Drama can be very engrossing for its participants and it is helpful for them to know what signals you are going to use when you want them to stop.

## Strategies – ways of working

You may notice in the topics some 'ways of working' that you have not come across before. This section gives a more detailed explanation of some of these strategies than is possible within the main text.

### Working in-role – teacher in-role

This may be a strategy that fills you with apprehension, but contrary to many teachers' initial fears, it does not require you to give a spectacular acting performance (which could, in fact, be counterproductive if the class looks upon it as something to sit back and watch rather than interact with). What is needed is, first, an attempt by the participant, whether child or teacher, to get inside the mind or way of thinking of the person/role being taken on. Then the attitudes, thoughts and feelings of the role need to be expressed verbally and in an appropriate way so that it helps all those involved to commit themselves seriously to the situation. For example, Mrs Besant in *Matchgirls* is likely to be concerned about finding out the exact conditions inside the factory and at the same time aware of the risks being taken by those workers who have agreed to meet her. Her behaviour, therefore, will probably be low-key and perhaps a little furtive; she will take trouble to reassure the workers that she was not followed and she may also be quite persistent in making sure she fully understands the answers they give. If, on the other hand, she used an inappropriate method of delivery – if she was loud and jovial or said things like 'OK you lot, just give me the low-down on old Bryant and Mays', everyone involved would find it very difficult to believe in the 'as if' situation being created. This may seem no more than common sense and in many ways it is, but

for the children taking part, who have not had the life experiences of an adult, this sort of work offers them a chance to 'meet' many new situations and people, try out ways of responding to them, and subsequently analyse and evaluate the outcomes in a supportive learning environment.

It is important that you approach all your work in-role seriously. The children will take their cue from you and if you indicate that it is all a bit of a laugh, or that you are not really committed to what you are doing, then you will almost certainly get the same sort of response from the class and it is unlikely that any learning will take place. You may feel that initially the class will find it difficult to accept you in any role other than that of the teacher, and it is often helpful to have a preliminary attempt at the strategy just to get used to seeing each other taking on new roles and practising picking up clues about who people are and what the situation is. For example, if your class is sitting on chairs you might approach some of them as a deck-chair attendant; they could pick up clues from such things as your requests for money and comments on things like the weather, the sand, and how long they have been on holiday. If, on the other hand, the children are all sitting round their tables in the classroom you could approach as a waiter and begin to take orders. These are likely to be fairly brief exchanges as everyone gets used to what is required of him or her, but once you and the class have got the hang of it you could try an extended interaction – a meeting to plan an occasion of some kind, for example, a school or church fête, or, more adventurously, a round-the-world yacht race! Another more physically active idea might be the preparation of the Christmas shop-window displays in a large department store. As chief window dresser, you can depute groups of employees to arrange the dummies (other class members) in a series of displays round a central theme. What is important is that everyone gets used to listening carefully. Then they can pick up and act appropriately on the information gathered from what others say and do.

Sometimes it is difficult to know quite how to begin, but it is usually helpful if everyone is aware that the drama is starting at a specific moment. You can try telling the class that you are going to move to another part of the room and that when you come back you will be playing someone else and the drama will have started, or you could get everyone positioned as if caught in a still photograph that comes alive at the click of your fingers.

Another method is to designate an invisible line, or screen, which once passed over, or through, takes you into the 'as if' world you are going to inhabit.

You will notice that there are times when it is suggested that you take on a specific role and others where there is a choice. This was really only a matter of expediency on my part when planning how best to present the topics and you, as the teacher, need to make your own decisions as to which role you feel would be most appropriate for you to adopt at any point, taking into consideration your own confidence and the roles you feel the children would benefit from playing.

If, for example, you have a class that has done a lot of drama and is confident in handling the medium, you may well feel that the best role for you is one with little power or status, so you could let a child or children take on the roles with those qualities. On the other hand, if you feel unsure of yourself in a new way of working you will probably want to take a role which gives you similar controls to those of a teacher. It really is a matter for your own judgement, and of course you do not have to stick with one role all the time. You may find yourself in a position where you feel the drama would be best served by the introduction of another role, in which case you can say things like: 'I'm just going to see if I can find . . .' or 'I have to go now. I might be back sometime but I'm not sure.' Then you can leave the drama and re-enter it in the new role: 'I just saw (name of character you were playing) in the street. S/he looked very worried. Has anything happened?' or 'Can you help me? I've only just arrived in this area and I'm looking for . . .'

You need to be aware of why you are choosing to play a particular role. You may wish, for example, to confront the group by putting difficulties in its path, or you may want to be a source of help and advice that the group can consult or perhaps you want to present them with someone who needs to be protected or aided in some way. There are very many different reasons for choosing your role and you will have to weigh up the needs of your class before making your choice.

In drama you can be anyone you want to be and that includes a member of the opposite sex. It has been my experience that a lot of girls will happily take on male roles but that many boys experience initial difficulty in adopting a female role with a serious attitude. However, provided it is approached sensitively and no one is

forced or rushed into it, I have found that with time this first response can be overcome and drama can then begin to make useful contributions to learning about gender issues.

The essence of role play is that you are sharing the experience with your class; it is something you create together. At the same time you, as the teacher, are constantly monitoring the learning that is taking place and looking for opportunities to extend the children's exploration of that experience, to deepen or change their understanding of it.

## Improvisation

This is what both you and the children might think of as 'acting' and to a certain extent you would be right. In improvisation we are pretending to be either someone other than ourselves or in a situation other than the one we are actually physically in, or both at the same time, and this, you would probably argue, is what an actor does. However, there are one or two differences which may not be immediately apparent but which make quite a difference to the experience. To begin with, most actors are interpreting someone else's words, but in improvisation the participants are both authors and interpreters of the words and actions; they have to decide both what to say and how to say it. The other element that is usually different (in spontaneous as opposed to planned improvisation) is the audience, or rather the lack of one. In acting, we are aiming to communicate to everyone 'out there', but in spontaneous improvisation the participants are usually only trying to communicate with each other. If you think about it you will see that this, in fact, mirrors life. We are the authors and interpreters of our own words and we are usually only trying to communicate with those to whom we are speaking. Therefore, improvisation can feel very 'real' and can be exciting and ultimately very enlightening if the opportunity is taken to analyse and evaluate the experience in a sensitive way.

Two kinds of improvisation were mentioned above: planned and spontaneous. The differences between them need to be understood by both you and the class.

## Planned improvisation

This is sometimes referred to as 'play making', which is a good description of what is entailed. The work

presupposes that you want to communicate something to another group of people (your audience) and in order to do that you need to stand outside the improvisation/ play that you create to see that it says what you want it to say. This almost inevitably involves a process of adjusting and altering until you are satisfied that your 'message' is as clear as you can make it.

Within the classroom this type of work is the one that your group is most likely to associate with 'drama'. It can be very useful in stimulating discussion provided everyone focuses on the 'message' and is concerned with the light the play throws on the problem or idea you are thinking about, rather than just talking about surface impressions such as 'That was good because it was funny' or 'I liked the bit where Hazel and Heather were fighting', while ignoring *why* the characters behaved as they did. This part of the process is vital. It is the time when you are interacting with the whole class and can help the children develop new understandings, so you need to make sure you do not have to rush through this section because you have run out of time.

As this way of working lays great emphasis on communication, things like being heard, making sure everyone can see important actions, shaping the improvisation so that it has a beginning, middle and end, and building towards climactic moments will all become important, so you may also wish to talk about these aspects after watching a play. It can become very frustrating for the participants if their lack of technical skills obstructs their ability to get their ideas across.

Finally, when the groups are working on their improvisations your input is important, so do not just leave them to get on with it. This is not easy as you cannot divide yourself into six or seven bits, but do try and visit as many groups as you can because your challenging of a superficial response or your thought-provoking question can help the group extend its thinking and make new discoveries. If you leave the groups to their own devices you are likely to get work of little depth, as the children have only their own limited experience to draw on and are unlikely to stretch themselves.

## Spontaneous improvisation

This way of working does not usually include an audience and the participants begin interacting with each other without pre-planning what will happen. They often need to have some background information before they begin, but from then on this kind of improvisation resembles life where we also interact with each other without stopping to plan what we will do next. This creation of a 'real' situation makes all sorts of demands on those taking part. They need to find appropriate language, to think on their feet, to make decisions, to meet any challenges that the teacher or others put in their way, and during the course of such encounters they can find their understanding being changed or deepened. In this form of improvisation it is the process that is all important; there will be no tangible end-product to look at but the members of the group will have experienced something together which they can then look back on and use as a resource to analyse, evaluate and discuss.

More experienced groups may decide to use this way of working to open up ideas as a preliminary stage to a planned improvisation, but it is likely to be used most by you when working in-role with the whole group creating the drama together.

## Discussion

This is perhaps the word used most in the topics and it fulfils two different functions. First, it is one way of exploring and discovering things that will be useful in the drama. Secondly, it is often used as a means of reflecting on and evaluating the class's experience. Where this is the case, you will find suggestions in the text for some of the points you might want to raise. As each drama is a unique event, however, only you and the children can ultimately decide which areas would be most profitable to probe. When using discussion for either function, your questions need to be open-ended and your position as neutral as possible so that the children are encouraged to contribute their own ideas, and their attitudes and feelings are explored without being overshadowed by your own.

## Hot seating

When hot seating a character, the group is able to question him/her in depth about motivations, feelings, life-style, family background and so on. This can obviously be a lot for a child to cope with and he/she must always know that he/she can stop at any time. There are other ways too of reducing the pressure. You can give the person in the hot seat the option of saying

'Swap' if he/she finds a question too difficult, in which case the person who asked the question changes places and tries to put him or herself in the hot seater's shoes and give an answer. Alternatively, as used in *Chemical Dump*, a group representing the thoughts and feelings of the character can offer the person in the hot seat advice which he/she may or may not take, or a group can collectively speak for one person, chipping in with things at any time in the interview. Finally, a whole group of people can be hot seated together as happens in *Evacuees*. In this case, because of the diverse nature of group members, the information gathered is probably going to be of a more generalised nature than in the other forms.

## Forum theatre

Using this method the class works as a whole on a problem. A group begins with either a spontaneous or planned improvisation and the rest of the class is invited to suggest alternative ways of dealing with the situation which the improvisers then try putting into practice. Alternatively, members of the class are given the opportunity to try out their ideas by taking over a role within the drama themselves. A further possibility is to allow the observers to stop the improvisation at any time to consider one specific point rather than deal with the thing as a whole. This can be useful if there seems to be a crucial moment when a decision might make a radical impact on the outcome.

## Reflection and evaluation

We have already looked at this in one form under the heading 'Discussion', but this vital element can also be approached from within the drama by, for example, writing or drawing in-role things like diaries, reports, letters, and working on the zoo plans in *Zoo Quest*, a task that entails evaluating that whole activity and so offers the potential for many new understandings to be reached. Characters thinking aloud, whether their thoughts are voiced by themselves or by a partner, or the use of still images as in *Citizenship* or *Chemical Dump*, are also times when reflection on past or present experience is taking place. It is interesting to note that in the use of still images, reflection can be expressed in a non-verbal way. Finally, there is discussion that takes place in-role as in the reporting back session in *Zoo Quest* or Mrs Besant's meeting with the matchworkers, where analysis, evaluation, and reflection may all find a place.

## Still images or freeze frame

These can help to bring an idea or feeling sharply into focus. Working to convey a message without dialogue can make the group think carefully about spatial relationships and what they say, about how symbols rather than words can be used to express a concept. It encourages the practice of interpreting images and can lead to exploration of the meanings that lie beneath the surface.

When first introducing this strategy, you may wish to get the class tuned in to this way of working. You could begin by asking them to imagine they were arguing in pairs when you took a photograph of them. What would it look like? Try it out and view some of the results. You can then talk about the body language and facial expressions being used and point out how we all understand these aspects of communication just as clearly as speech. You can then try other interactions such as one or both participants being upset by someone or something or perhaps being pleased or doubtful. Moving on, you might ask them to show a moment of discovery. Is it clear where the object of discovery is? What tells us? How subtle can we make our signals and still convey the message? Do we know what each person's reaction to the discovery is? How? In these simple exercises the class is learning to focus the observer's attention and to convey information about feelings and relationships, all without the use of verbal language.

## Mantle of the expert

This strategy, developed originally by Dorothy Heathcote, places the participants in a 'knowing' role where their possession of a particular expertise enables them to deal with a situation from a position of authority. The benefits to be gained are the serious attitude and sense of self-worth generated by the status with which the participants are invested, and the stimulus the role provides to acquire their expert's knowledge. This task-oriented strategy has wide-ranging applications. Within the topics in this book the children are offered the opportunity to become, among other things, nutritionists, health workers, zoologists, environmentalists and water engineers, but, allied to other topics, they could just as easily be exploring the world of the town planner, archaeologist, hotelier or architect.

# National Curriculum

With the advent of the National Curriculum, all teachers are naturally interested to know in what way an idea or method of working can aid its implementation. When drama is used as a learning medium, it can contribute towards the following:

- The development of language, both oral and written, by providing a context which stimulates a need to question, instruct, persuade, argue, advise, convince, use a different register and so on.

- The development of understanding of different points of view, by employing role play and simulations which allow experimentation within a controlled yet 'real' situation, and which incorporate both reflection and evaluation in some form as a matter of course.

- Providing the child with opportunities to solve problems and evaluate the outcomes in many different contexts; to look at the implications behind actions and speech; to use thought to plan, predict, imagine, speculate, decide and make moral choices.

- Stimulating the need to know and consequently, depending on the context chosen (historical, environmental, scientific etc.), provide a powerful incentive for research and information gathering.

- Enabling both groups and individuals to function together successfully, balancing the needs of all concerned; learning to compromise, negotiate and work productively with others.

The topics in this book are primarily aimed at pupils working at Key Stage 2, although many activities will be found suitable for both Key Stage 1 and the first years of Key Stage 3.

# Attainment Targets

The following guide indicates the Attainment Targets that can be addressed in each topic.

### Attainment Targets

| ORAL FLUENCY | |
|---|---|
| English | 1 |

| ZOO QUEST | |
|---|---|
| English | 1, 3 |
| Geography | 1, 2, 3, 4, 5 |
| Science | 1, 2, 3 |
| Technology | 1, 2, 3, 4 |

| FAMINE | |
|---|---|
| English | 1, 2, 3 |
| Geography | 1, 2, 3, 4, 5 |
| Maths | 1, 2, 3, 8, 11 |
| Science | 1, 2, 3, 5, 9, 13, 14 |
| Technology | 1, 2, 3, 4 |

| CHEMICAL DUMP | |
|---|---|
| English | 1, 2, 3 |
| Geography | 4, 5 |
| Science | 1, 2, 5, 9, 14 |
| Technology | 1, 2, 3, 4 |

| CITIZENSHIP | |
|---|---|
| English | 1 |
| Maths | 1, 9, 11 |
| Science | 1, 5 |

### Attainment Targets

| CASTLES AND VILLAGE LIFE | |
|---|---|
| English | 1, 2, 3 |
| Geography | 1, 4 |
| History | 1, 3 |
| Maths | 8 |
| Technology | 1, 2, 3, 4 |

| MATCHGIRLS | |
|---|---|
| English | 1, 3 |
| Geography | 4 |
| History | 1, 2, 3 |
| Science | 1, 3 |
| Technology | 1 |

| EVACUEES | |
|---|---|
| English | 1, 3 |
| Geography | 1 |
| History | 1, 2, 3 |
| Maths | 1, 8, 11 |
| Science | 1 |
| Technology | 1, 2, 3, 4 |

*Throughout the book, comments intended only for the teacher are printed in italics.*

*This section, dealing with talking, listening and expressing ideas and arguments clearly and successfully, is a useful preparation for many of the activities used in the main topics.*

*The ideas here can be taken in isolation or can be inserted as part of the work on a specific section, in which case you could adapt the content to the topic being undertaken. For example, if you were to use 'Group stories' in preparation for the stories in **Castles and Village Life**, you could suggest objects to be introduced such as a sword, a herd of pigs and a castle moat. In **Famine** the objects could be a mountain, two elephants and a mask.*

*In addition, you might like to use some of these activities to work towards making 'radio programmes' which you could record.*

*Some ideas:*

## Interviews

- With 'celebrities'
  - real
  - fictional

Prime Minister

pop star

- With historical characters

Elizabeth I      Julius Caesar      Florence Nightingale

- Impromptu interviews by a roving reporter

## Discussions of news items, opinions

### Weather reports

### National and local news

## Programme introductions

### Story reading, story telling

## Games

Radio and TV provide many ideas which you could use. For example: *Just a Minute, Hoax, Call My Bluff.*

CHILDREN'S WORLD

## Group stories

In groups of three to five, make up a story with each person contributing one sentence and then passing it on to the next person.

The story can be given a theme:

'Into space'

or

an opening sentence: 'They watched warily as the smoke curled upwards, then . . .'

or

each person in the group can be given something to introduce into the story. This can be done openly, or secretly so that no one knows anyone else's item.

### Possible developments

- *No one may bring in his or her 'item' during the first round.*
- *People can challenge if they think they know the object someone is trying to introduce. If they are correct, that person is out.*

## Talking your partner to a standstill

In pairs, talk at each other until one of you stops!

You can have a set subject which everyone talks about, or each person can choose his or her own.

Let the ones left talking pair up and try again.

Those who stopped first can pair up and have another go.

### Looking at what happened

Why did some people stop? Did they run out of things to say? Did they feel overpowered by their partner? Why? Was it loudness? Speed? Interesting content? Physical dominance? Were they distracted?

---

Think about the differences between talking *at* and talking *with*.

To talk *with* you need to:

● Take turns

*Well, I'd say . . .*

*So what do you think?*

● Actively listen, bodily and vocally

*And then his mum came in!*

*Ohhh.*

*zzzz*

● Respond appropriately

*You'll never guess what happened then.*

*Did you see Top of the Pops yesterday?*

*No, what? Go on, tell me.*

In groups of three, two talk together and one observes. Did the talkers leave space for their partners to speak? Did they encourage their partners? How? Did they seem interested in what their partner said? How did they show it?

---

## Explaining

Explain a simple process to your partner or to the whole group. For example, making a bed:

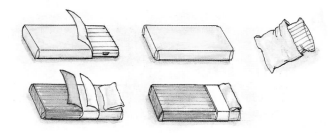

Did you get things in the right order? Did you sound as if you knew what you were talking about? Did you use gestures? Were they helpful?

### Other ideas

● Making a cup of tea
● Catching a bus
● Cleaning your teeth

## Describe and draw

*Gather a group of objects that the class cannot see. One class member – out of sight of the rest of the class – is given one of the objects. His or her task is to describe the object, while the class attempts to draw it. Compare the drawings with the object.*

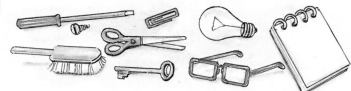

### Possible developments

● *Describer must not mention what the object does or what it is made of.*
● *The class may not ask for clarification.*
● *Describer may not watch the class as it draws.*

*Discuss the problems that arose.*

# INTERVIEWS

## Who might be involved?

Employee

Employer

Expert

Celebrity

Programme presenter

Reporter

Members of the public

Headteacher

Pupil

## What are interviews for?

- To find out information.
- To get someone's point of view.
- To bring something to someone's attention.
- To stir people to action.
- To clarify situations.

## What are the problems that can arise?

Replies that are not detailed enough.

Nurse Shaw, tell us about your job.

Well, I make lots of beds.

Questions that can be answered by just *yes* or *no*.

Have you found the local neighbours helpful?

Yes.

## Yes/No question game

*Ask each participant a question which could have a* yes *or* no *answer. Responders must answer without saying* yes *or* no.

### Some questions

- Are you eleven?
- Do you like sausages?
- Have you got a pet?
- Do you watch TV every day?
- Can you swim?
- Are chips your favourite food?
- Do you play football?
- Have you been abroad?
- Do you think school holidays are too long?
- If I offered you £100, would you take it?

## Constructing helpful questions

*The children attempt to ask you questions to which you cannot give* yes *or* no *as an answer. For example:*

- How would you feel if school holidays were shortened?
- What do you particularly like about your favourite foods?
- If I gave you £100, what would you spend it on?

In pairs, try the same activity again.
First, attempt to catch your partner out:

Can you ride a bike?

I've been meaning to learn, but I haven't got around to it yet.

Then try to prevent your partner saying *yes* or *no*:

Do tell me about your visit to York.

Well, we began by going to the Jorvik Viking Centre.

# Getting across a point of view

*Arguing both sides of a case is useful practice for working in-role.*

## Whole group

Choose a topic. For instance, 'Wearing school uniform'.

## Pick out the main points:

**FOR**

It makes the whole school feel they belong together.

There's no time wasted choosing what to wear.

**AGAINST**

It prevents people feeling like individuals.

You end up having two sets of clothes.

**FOR**

It cuts down competition over dress.

**AGAINST**

Other clothes are more comfortable when you're working and being active.

## Wearing school uniform

### In pairs

**Round 1:**

As argue *for*

Bs argue *against*

**Round 2:**

As argue *against*

Bs argue *for*

## Discussion

Who had a good argument? Why was it good? Who found it harder to argue for something they disagreed with? Why? Did you sound unconvincing? Did anyone find it easier? Why? Were you calmer because you didn't feel strongly?

## You could also try arguments

In whispers

Very loudly

One quietly, one loudly

With a time limit

In threes, two against one

## Other topics to try

- *Sweets should be rationed.*
- *The hours that children watch TV should be restricted.*
- *School holidays are too long.*

# PREPARATION

## Pre-expedition meeting

*The teacher, in-role as Expedition Leader, welcomes experts (children) in the fields of: Nutrition (food), Botany (plants), Zoology (animals).*

## The Expedition Leader outlines the main aim

To look at animals in their natural habitats in order to reproduce similar conditions in our zoos.

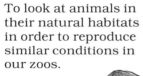

Environment
Food
Quality of
life

The experts are asked to introduce themselves to their neighbours and tell them about their special knowledge of food, plants or animals.

## Possible development

*Neighbours introduce each other to the rest of the group.*

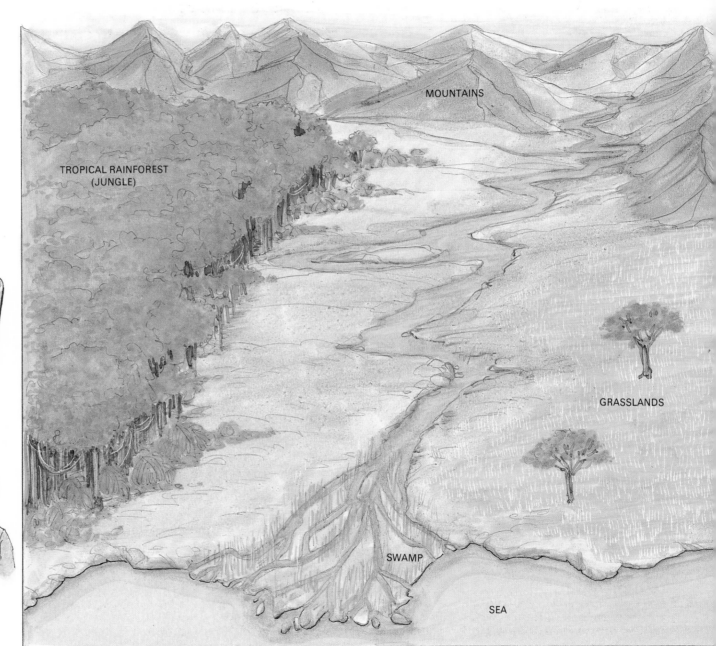

MOUNTAINS

TROPICAL RAINFOREST (JUNGLE)

GRASSLANDS

SWAMP

SEA

## The map

### Options

- *The teacher makes a map.*
- *Each child can have a photocopy of the map opposite.*
- *The children can create a map.*
- *You can use a real map.*

## Consulting the map

### Types of questions

- What kinds of animals and insects could we find in this swampy area?
- Do we have an expert here who knows about swamps?
- In your opinion, do you think we will find crocodiles here?
- From your knowledge of rainforests, what do you expect we'll find in this area?
- Are there any insects or animals that we might have to be extra careful about? Why?

## Planning the landing

Divide into groups, with a variety of experts in each one.

Each group needs to consider the best place to land. Then have a general discussion and make a whole-group decision.

## Possible methods of transport

| | Advantages? | Disadvantages? |
|---|---|---|
| aeroplane | • Speed | • Noisy<br>• No landing strip<br>• Limited cargo space |
| airship | • Quiet | • Limited cargo space<br>• Landing difficulties |
| ship | • Large cargo space<br>• Quiet | • Slow<br>• No harbour |

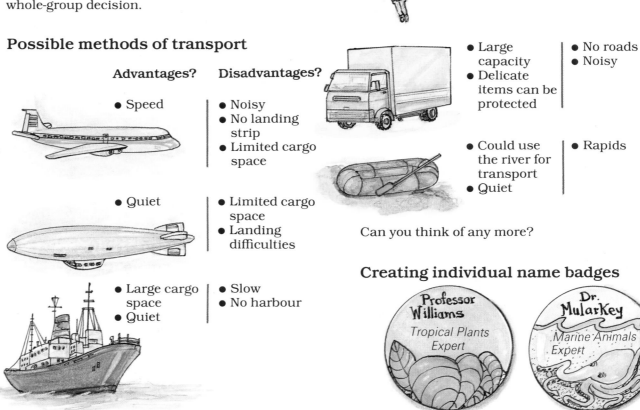

| | Advantages? | Disadvantages? |
|---|---|---|
| hot air balloon | • No landing strip needed<br>• Quiet | • Small fuel reserves<br>• Uncontrolled landing |
| parachute | • Can land on difficult terrain<br>• Quiet | • Training needed<br>• Problems with delicate or very large items |
| truck | • Large capacity<br>• Delicate items can be protected | • No roads<br>• Noisy |
| boat | • Could use the river for transport<br>• Quiet | • Rapids |

Can you think of any more?

## Creating individual name badges

Professor Williams — *Tropical Plants Expert*

Dr. Mularkey — *Marine Animals Expert*

# PRACTISING SKILLS

The experts decide which skills are needed for a successful expedition:

*Moving carefully.*

*Listening well.*

*Moving silently.*

*Noticing things.*

## Moving carefully

Half the group represents trees.
The other half moves among the trees without touching them.

The trees can be moved closer together to make training harder.

*Chairs could also be used to represent trees.*

*Paper squares representing obstacles can increase the difficulties.*

## Listening well

### Identifying sounds

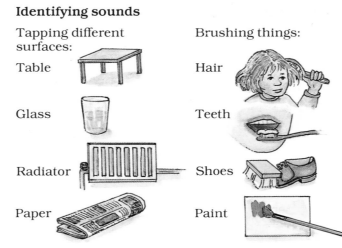

Tapping different surfaces:

Table

Glass

Radiator

Paper

Brushing things:

Hair

Teeth

Shoes

Paint

Alternatively, you could make a recording of animal sounds to be identified.

## Moving silently

Can you cross the room without being heard by a blindfolded listener?

Add more listeners in the centre. Now, as listeners, can you also feel people passing you? To move silently, is it better to go quickly or slowly?

## Noticing things

A group of 4 or 5 takes up a position. The rest of the experts are given time to look, then they close their eyes.

The group changes position. The experts look again and try to identify changes.

*Repeat this with other groups and gradually make fewer and fewer or smaller and smaller changes.*

### Other ideas

A variation of *Grandmother's Footsteps:*

One member of the class represents a wild animal with acute hearing. The expedition members move silently and carefully forward, freezing whenever 'the animal' turns round. If 'the animal' sees any expert moving, that expert must go back to the start.

A variation of *Keeper of the Keys:*

How near to the wild animal can you get? See who can sit nearest without being heard.

*To make this harder, you can add a barrier of obstacles to be negotiated.*

# EQUIPMENT

## What equipment will we need?

### In pairs

Make a list. You could draw the items.

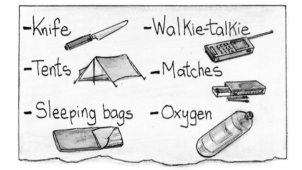

### Whole class

Now pool all the ideas.

Tick off each item on your list as it is mentioned. Add to your list anything that you forgot.

You could have a discussion about which items are the most important ones to take, and why.

## Individually

Think of the special things you will need to do your job.

Ms Wood
**Soil Scientist**

Professor Richardson
**Tropical Plants Expert**

Dr Travis
**Swamp Insects Expert**

## Packing the equipment

Use imaginary things. Some items will need very careful packing.

## Assembling and loading cargo

Make one big stack, then think of the best way to load it on to the transport.

One idea could be a human chain.

Which other ways can you think of?

## Pre-expedition group photograph for the local paper

*You can take either a real photograph or an imaginary one.*

While you're having your photograph taken, think about how you feel. Are you excited, worried, happy, sad? Why?

## ON THE EXPEDITION

Things you could do:

### Choosing where to camp

*How about here?*

*No, the ground's too wet.*

*This looks a good place, the trees will give us shelter.*

### Setting up camp

Some questions that could arise:

How shall we arrange the tents?
Have you erected a tent before?
How shall we start?
Who's going to hammer in the pegs?
Is the ground soft enough?

### Unpacking personal belongings

What's in your bags?
Where will you put your things?

*I'm going to use this packing case as a cupboard – do you want to share it?*

### Waking up on the first morning

*Narration and mime can be used to examine what the children think, feel, do and hear.*

*Some ideas for your narration:*

What can you hear? Listen to the sounds outside your tent.

Snake

Cockatoo

Lion

Elephant

Cricket

*You could use a recording of real animal sounds or let the children imagine them.*

Is the sun up yet? Is it hot in your tent? How did you sleep? Were you excited? Are you looking forward to today? Let your mind run back over last evening/your arrival/when you said goodbye to your family.

It's time to get up. Where are you going to wash?

In a stream?

In a plastic bowl?

In a canvas wash-basin?

Now you can get dressed, putting on the special clothes you brought for exploring. Perhaps . . .

Long trousers to protect your legs?

Or shorts to keep you cool?

A lightweight jacket with lots of pockets?

Or a warm jacket for climbing the mountains?

Thigh-length waders for the swamp?

Climbing boots?

Trainers for protection and walking?

Open sandals?

A soft hat for the sun?

A helmet for climbing?

## Issuing equipment

You could use imaginary things.

*Can you help me with the inflatable boat?*

*Can I have the portable microscope?*

*This will need careful handling.*

Or you could make some equipment.

Binoculars

Microscope

Camera

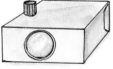

Soil sample container

Two-way radio

## Do we need to check our equipment?

Are my binoculars working?

Is the microphone picking up sounds?

Is there a film in my camera?

Are my knives sharp?

*Can you hear me? Over and out.*

Is the tranquilliser gun loaded? Have we got any spare cartridges?

## Taking pictures and filming

Do we need to practise?
How will we get the best angles?

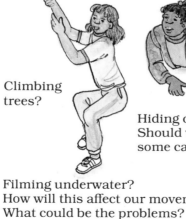

Climbing trees?

Crawling through the undergrowth?

Hiding ourselves? Should we make some camouflage?

Filming underwater?
How will this affect our movement?
What could be the problems?
How can we solve them?

## Safety

Everyone needs to leave a record of where he or she is going.

| Mountains | Swamp | Rainforest | Sea |
|---|---|---|---|
| Dr. Patel | Dr. Travis | Prof. Williams Prof. Richardson | Dr. Mularkey |

## Final briefing

Remember:

Move quietly

Walk carefully

Look and listen

## Exploration

Individually?

In pairs?

*Did you say you can see two?*

In groups?

*Crocodiles to our right . . .*

# REPORTING BACK

At a formal camp meeting?

Around the camp fire?

Over a meal?

## Issues that could arise

- The question of whether we are disturbing the animals too much.
- The problems of maintaining safety without guns.
- Ideas for improving the life of zoo animals, based on what has been observed.
- The sighting of a previously unknown animal or insect:
  Does this alter our attitude?
  Do we capture it?
  Do we photograph or film it?
  Do we tell others?
  What will be the outcome of our actions?

## Diaries

*Diary entries can be used at any stage that seems appropriate.*

July 28th

We have arrived. We landed by parachute this afternoon. The equipment seems to be OK but we haven't unpacked it all yet. We put up the tents first and had a meal. Now I'm very sleepy so will stop writing for today. Tomorrow I'm off to the mountains...

July 30th

Have just returned from the mountains.

## Returning expedition members give interviews

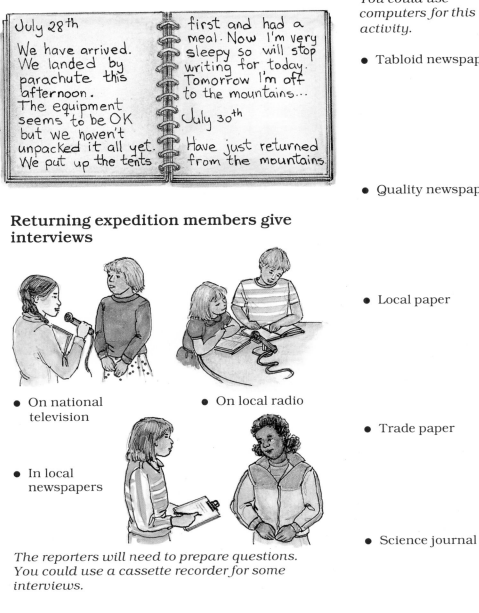

- On national television
- On local radio
- In local newspapers

*The reporters will need to prepare questions. You could use a cassette recorder for some interviews.*

## Newspaper articles can be written in different styles

*You could use computers for this activity.*

- Tabloid newspaper
- Quality newspaper
- Local paper
- Trade paper
- Science journal

**THE SUN**

**Dramatic discovery in the jungle!**

Scientists returning from a four-week jaunt in the African jungle

**THE INDEPENDENT**

**Experts could have good news for zoos**

Twenty-four experts in various fields returned from

**SMITHAM REPORTER**

**Exciting trip for Kathy**

Local biologist Kathy Roberts returned last week from a trip to Africa

**ZOO NEWS**

**Frampton Zoo to get a face-lift?**

Experts returning from a fact-finding trip to Africa have been

**SCIENCE NOW**

**New environmental clues**

New evidence has been put forward which shows that

# IMPLEMENTING IDEAS

## Replanning a zoo

Do we keep the same number of species?

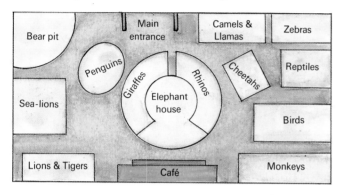

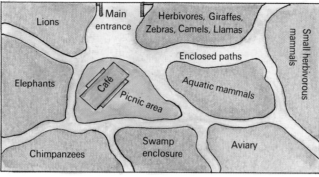

## Replanning an enclosure

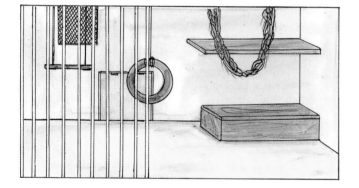

## Replanning feeding routines

Could animals use tools to obtain their food?

## A 'slide' show

*This could be a way of sharing the expedition's discoveries with others, using tableaux for the slides plus a commentary.*

*This topic deals with some of the issues that arise when a community has to cope with disaster.*

*The class will gain experience in decision making – developing the skills of consultation, discernment, judgment and consideration. The work encourages the growth of empathic understanding by making demands for appropriate responses – both verbal and non-verbal – from two very different groups of people.*

*There are also rich opportunities to explore aesthetic awareness and understanding through personal creative work, particularly in the sections on ceremonies and myths.*

## Values

*This first activity gives the class a picture of themselves against which they can place their discoveries about a very different group of people.*

### Individually

On separate pieces of paper, write the two things you most value in life. One should be a concrete object or thing and the other an abstract feeling or condition.

*Collect these papers in two separate piles and set aside. They do not need to be discussed at this stage.*

## Thinking about food and hunger

**In pairs**

Describe to each other the best meal you can imagine. Think of how it looks, tastes and smells.

## Exploration of hunger

### Whole group

Who has ever been hungry? What did it feel like?

After describing the feeling in words, find a way for your body to describe it. Try this individually, then in pairs or groups.

Talk about how we understand the things our bodies say; how we use:

Our faces        Our hands        Our bodies
                 and arms

*This next section moves from a whole-group discussion to a teacher-led narration and mime sequence and finally into a spontaneous improvisation.*

*If the class has not worked with you in-role before, let them know that you will be joining in.*

## Discussion

We're going to try and imagine what it's like to live in a very different country.

| Here | There |
|------|-------|
|  |  |
| Shops for all our needs | No shops |
| 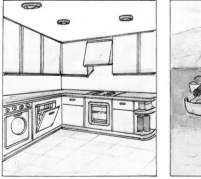 |  |
| Electricity | No electricity |

| Here | There |
|------|-------|
| 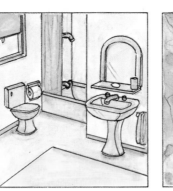 | |
| Clean running water | No running water |
|  | |
| Transport and roads | No roads or transport |

Shall we try to become some villagers living in this different land?

## Narration and mime sequence

*An idea of the kind of thing you could say:*

On your own, find a space and sit down.
Now close your eyes. You are going to begin by making a picture inside your head.

Imagine . . . no rain has fallen on our village for a whole year. So all our crops have shrivelled and died and now we are eating the last of our food.

See yourself in your picture. You are a mother or father and at the moment you are gathering up the very last of your food supplies to feed to your child.

Perhaps you are weak because you haven't eaten for some time. You are probably very hungry, but your child comes first. See yourself . . . maybe bending over a large storage jar . . .

or carefully picking the last grains of corn out of a sack.

You are going to prepare the food for your child by yourself. Perhaps you need to peel and chop it, or grind it so that it can be mixed to a paste. When the food is ready, you are going to feed it to your child. (You can imagine the child.)

As soon as you have a picture in your head, begin to gather your food. Don't watch anyone else, just concentrate on what you are doing.

When you have finished, lay down your child and come and sit by me.

*The teacher is working alongside the class.*

## Spontaneous improvisation

*The whole group with the teacher in-role as a villager.*

*As the group gathers round . . .*

> That's the last of my food gone. I feel so helpless. I don't know what to do next, do you?

*Still in-role, explore feelings and possible courses of action.*

*You might want to retain the leadership yourself or you could pass it on to a child or a group of children:*

> Joanna, as our head villager, what do you think we should do?

*Whether as leader or not, the teacher in-role needs to be prepared to challenge the group to stimulate further thought:*

> If our elders had been wise, they would have told us to move before this happened. It's all their fault.

> How can we move away? The nearest town is a 50-mile walk.

> The very old, the sick, and the young. Should we take them or leave them behind?

> What if our strongest members went further afield to search for food and brought it back to us?

## Looking back

*In building belief, it is often helpful to examine the past as well as the present and future.*

## Film clips

### In groups

Five years ago, film-makers made a documentary about the village. They were particularly interested in the ceremonies, celebrations and rites of passage.

Create clips from the film, with each clip no longer than 60 seconds.

A wedding?

Death?

Hunting?

Celebrating the harvest?

Birth?

The coming of spring?

Becoming an adult?

Religion?

Watch each other's clips and then discuss the old life.

# FULL CEREMONY OR RITE

*This is a possible development.*

As a class, decide what your ceremony is for.
Your film clips might have given you some ideas.

## How is it going to begin?

With:

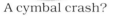

A cymbal crash?

A drumbeat?

A circle?

Two lines?

A procession?

## How does the ceremony progress?

Does one person lead?

Do different people or groups take it in turns?

Are the men and women separate or together?

## How does the ceremony end?

With:

Offerings to the gods?

Feasting?

Symbolic farewells?

## Will the ceremony include dancing?

What is the aim of the dance?
Is it to make people feel:

Happy?

Fierce?

United?

One group could make up the dance and teach it to the others.

## Will the dance need accompaniment?

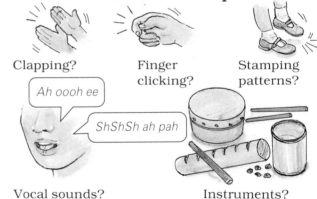

Clapping?

Finger clicking?

Stamping patterns?

*Ah oooh ee*

*ShShSh ah pah*

Vocal sounds?

Instruments?

A group could make some of the instruments.

## Will the ceremony need chants or songs?

Another group could devise these.

## Decorative objects for the ceremony

When food is plentiful, there is time to spend on aesthetic things.

Does the ceremony require special objects?

Can they be made?

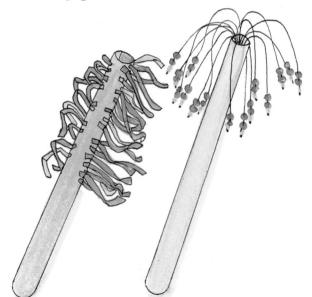

**Decorated clay pots, bowls and jugs**

**Ceremonial staffs or sceptres**

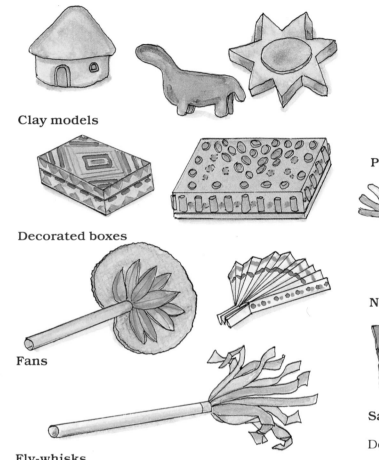

**Clay models**

**Decorated boxes**

**Fans**

**Fly-whisks**

Do the participants wear anything special?

**Decorated head-dresses**

**Painted masks**

**Necklaces and arm bracelets**

**Sashes**

Do they do their hair in a particular way?

*If the class is working in-role as they make these things, do they use any special words or charms as they work?*

# MYTHS AND LEGENDS

*This is a possible development.*

*Myths and legends take us even further back into the people's past. They could be devised and told in several different ways:*

- *A story in mime and movement. A narration could be added.*
- *Stories around the night fire, told by one person or a pair. There could be opportunities for the whole group to join in.*
- *Plays created by small groups, which are then shared with the whole group.*
- *Collective drawing on a large frieze depicting one or more legends.*

### How the gods made the animals

### How the first people came to this place

### The life after death

*Seeing the village from another point of view.*

# AID WORKERS

## What does this village need?

### Immediate relief aid?

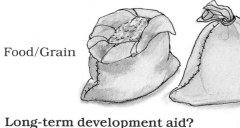

Food/Grain

### Long-term development aid?

Clean water

Irrigation

Sanitation

Improved farming methods

Health care

Storage for food/grain

Prevention of soil erosion

Improvement of livestock

Can you think of any others?

## Finding out

### In pairs or small groups

Choose which kind of expert you will be. Find out as much as you can about your particular area, so that you can present your information on the TV programme 'Aid' – *what is it?*

*Teacher in-role as a programme presenter*

*Hello and welcome. Development aid – what is it? I'm joined this evening by a number of experts who are going to put us in the picture. My first guests are . . .*

You may have prepared some diagrams, posters or models to help with your explanations.

*And here we have a small replica of a woven grain-storage bin.*

*At this point you could divide the class in two:*

### Villagers

Draw a plan of your village and its location.

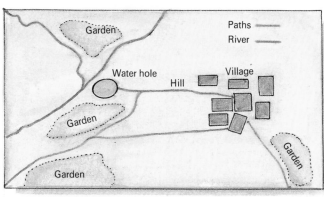

How many people live here?

Decide which crops you used to grow and which animals you kept.

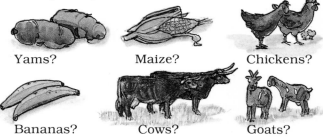

Yams?  Maize?  Chickens?

Bananas?  Cows?  Goats?

Why were they important?

### Aid workers

Prepare a list of questions to help you find out about the village and its needs.

In the old days . . .

Were you able to water your plants?

How many cattle did you have?

How often were people ill?

Get an idea of what it will cost to build a grain store or sink a well. Can you design an irrigation scheme that is cheap but effective and can be looked after easily by the villagers?

## Meeting of villagers and aid workers

*You could try spontaneous improvisation here, as everyone has a lot of background information.*

**Villagers:** create a still image showing life as it is in the village now.

**Aid workers:** collect your questions and prepare to enter the village.

I wonder who's going to speak first?

*You can use a sound such as a 'finger click' or a tambour to start everyone off.*

*You might find that a large village meeting evolves or that people split into small groups.*

## Possible developments
### An account of the meeting

In writing

| | |
|---|---|
| *Visitors came to the village today, they looked very fat.* | August 10th. Village of . . .<br><br>Information gathered<br>1. Water sources |
| **Villager** | **Aid worker** |

Or orally

- Telling a relation from another village

- Reporting back to a superior

### Discussing the results
#### Whole group

Compare the reactions and understanding of each group. Were they similar? If there were differences, why do you think they occurred? Did both groups find the meeting helpful? Were there any difficulties? If so, what might have caused them? Could they have been avoided?

## Budgeting

Either working as a whole class or divided into two groups – villagers and aid workers – decide how to allocate the money.

| Money available for village   £ _____ | | |
|---|---|---|
| **Cost of aid initiatives in** | **Money** | **Labour** |
| Clean water supply | _____ | _____ |
| Irrigation | _____ | _____ |
| Sanitation | _____ | _____ |
| Weekly health worker | _____ | _____ |
| Food/grain store | _____ | _____ |
| Soil conservation | _____ | _____ |
| Livestock improvement | _____ | _____ |

Find out the costs involved in making these 'improvements'. Decide which ones you will choose, and why.

Discuss with the other group your choices and the reasons for making them.

## Values

*You might like to ask the group to repeat the first activity in this topic (see page 20) in-role as the villagers.*

## Discussion

Are the values that emerge similar or very different? Why do you think this is?

*This topic examines the impact on a village community when it is proposed that a disused local gravel pit is sold to a waste disposal company.*

*There are opportunities to look at the proposal from both a pro and anti viewpoint, and to recognise that there are probably no straightforward 'right' solutions but that compromise, a willingness to negotiate, and settling for less than 100 per cent success are often the best ways to deal with real-life problems. The participants also have a strong incentive to 'find out' about the topic in order to make the drama work.*

*Possible ways in:*

## Teacher narrative

Rather like the opening passage of a story, there needs to be . . .

● **Some description of the village**

● **Details of people who live and work there**

Farmers and their families

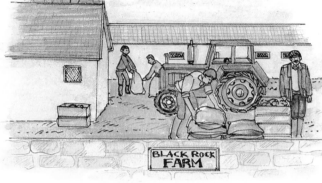

Farm workers and their families

Commuters and their families

The retired

Local traders and their families

● **Some idea of the potential problem**

MOODY'S GRAVEL

GRAVEL OF G.H.

ACQUIRED BY GETRID

## Newspaper cuttings

*You can use one or all of these depending on how much information you wish the children to find out for themselves.*

*The letter on its own, for example, leaves a great deal to be discovered and the class will need to decide how they go about this. One way could be to interview the owner of Moody's gravel pit (the teacher could take on this role).*

### HEATH ADVERTISER

Wednesday July 17th 1991

**LETTERS**

#### MYSTERY AT GREAT HAMPTON

Am I the only person in Great Hampton who saw the troop of London types poking around Moody's gravel pit last Tuesday morning?

They seemed to be taking samples from the pit bottom. What's going on?. That's what I want to know.

*S. Sargent*

Valley Cottage
Great Hampton

**ACCESS PROBLEMS**

and took four radios from the shop. He was remanded on bail until August 20th.

#### VILLAGERS GIVEN THE 'BRUSH OFF'

A small group of business-suited men clambering around Moody's old gravel pit provoked some interest in the village of Great Hampton last week.

On making enquiries, local householders were told only that the men were 'looking around'. No information was given as to who they were or why they were there. Some villagers feel unhappy about the 'brush off' they got from Mr George Moody who declined to say any more and who subsequently refused all our approaches saying that there was no information of any interest available at the moment. Many of the Great Hampton villagers would disagree with him there!

**HUNT IS ON FOR THE**

**Newsdesk: Heath 654**
**Classified Ads: Heath 922**
**Display Ads: Heath 655**

### HEATH ADVERTISER

Wednesday July 31st 1991               25p

## WASTE DUMP FOR GREAT HAMPTON?

Great Hampton has been thrown into turmoil by the news, released this week, that the waste disposal company Getrid is interested in buying Moody's disused gravel pit on the outskirts of the village.

Getrid, well-known for its recent policy of expansion after having taken over several smaller companies during the past two years, has contracts for the disposal of household, chemical and nuclear waste. Villagers are therefore understandably worried at the prospect of their quiet village being invaded by fleets of lorries and trucks bringing waste to the site. A Getrid spokesperson we managed to contact said there was no cause for alarm. Past experience has shown that by the ... this week

## Village map

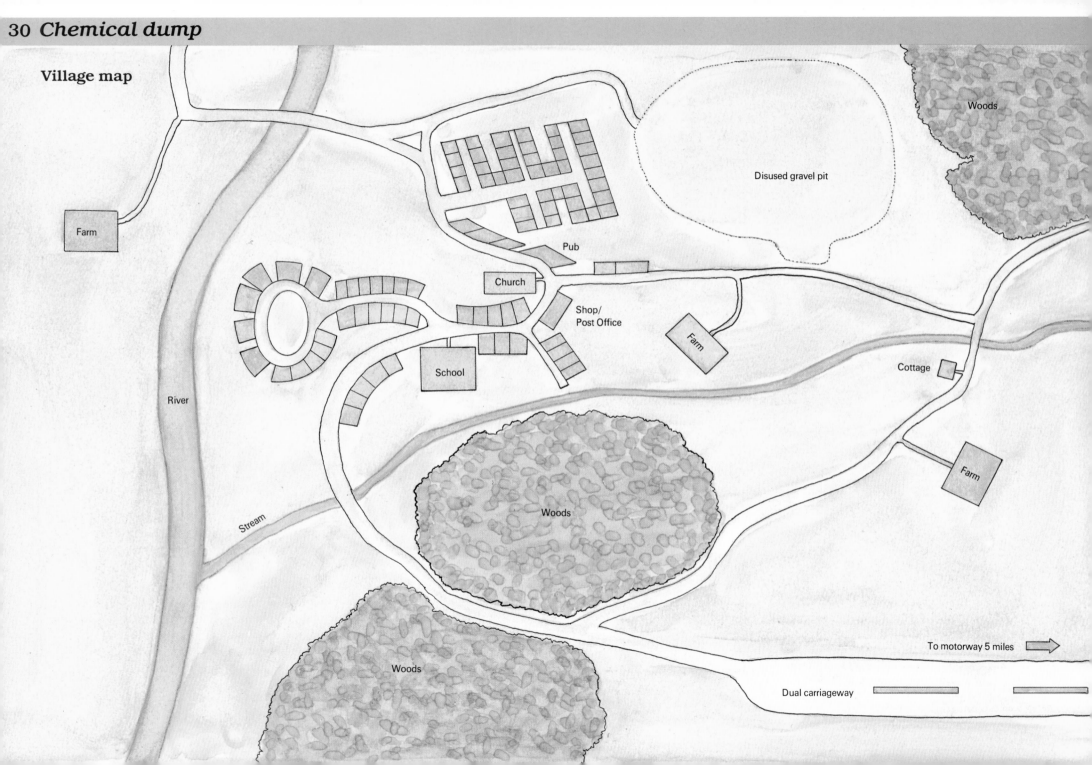

Farm

Disused gravel pit

Woods

Pub

Church

Shop/
Post Office

Farm

Cottage

School

Farm

River

Woods

Stream

Woods

To motorway 5 miles

Dual carriageway

## Village map

*The map on the opposite page has been drawn in such a way that you or the class can make decisions about names and who lives where. Alternatively, you could create your own map.*

Who are likely to be the interested parties? You could:

### Brainstorm together

Manager of Getrid.

Parents – they'll be worried about the increased traffic.

Environmental experts.

The unemployed – Getrid may bring jobs.

Mr. Moody
Farmers
The Vicar
The Publican
Local Councillors
Village shop Owner

Newcomers to the village and people who've retired to the village for peace and quiet.

## Or prepare role cards

**Seth Owen**
Farmer

**Sheila Hudd**
Headteacher

**Rev. Grant**

**Jack King**
Unemployed

You are 21.
Your father works for Seth Owen but you can't get a job.

**Carol King**
Housewife

You and your husband were born in the village. You are angry because there is no job for your son.

*You could put minimal information on these cards and then allow the class to supply all further ideas, or you could make them quite detailed. Everyone should take on a role.*

## Fleshing out the roles

### Individually

Write a short description of yourself.

Stan Wells
Publican

I'm a cheerful sort of person, always telling jokes and laughing. I get on with most people, which is just as well in my job.

Draw a picture of yourself.

## Or in pairs

We only moved here last year. I get a bit lonely sometimes.

Tell your partner about yourself.

I'd like you to meet Jane Cobb. She and her husband moved here last year.

Let your partner introduce you to the group.

## Whole group

Using the map, discuss who might be *for* (pro) and who might be *against* (anti) Getrid taking over the gravel pit, and why.

### Pro

Mr Moody?
Manager of Getrid?
Local councillors?
Unemployed?

### Is anyone neutral?

The vicar?

### Anti

The retired?
Newcomers?
Environmentalists?
Farmers?
Local councillors?

Divide into *pro* and *anti* groups.

## Action meetings

*Pro* and *anti* groups work in-role, with each planning a course of action.

### Local radio?

How can we make sure our point of view is aired?

### Local papers?

Do we need to do anything? Or do we leave it to the reporters?

What other forms of publicity shall we use?

**Car stickers?**

**T-shirts?**

**Celebrities?**

**Balloons?**

**Badges?**

**A protest march?**

**Leaflets?**

**Posters?**

### Whole group

Look at what has happened so far.

Did each group organise itself in the same way?
Are both groups using the same kind of strategies?
Can we foresee any problems arising?

Pressure groups can set up working parties to make:

**Badges**

**Posters**

Jobs

Homes

Peace of mind

GETRID WILL BRING THEM ALL

DO YOU WANT TO GETRID OF...
– wildlife?
– peace and quiet?
– clean air?

HANDS OFF OUR GRAVEL PIT

**Leaflets**

**Your help is needed to work for work.**

Support the campaign to bring Getrid to Great Hampton.

**Great Hampton gravel pit**

Think about what it could become. A lake for wild fowl and water sports.

**Banners**

Don't bury our jobs, bury the rubbish!

Good riddance to bad rubbish! Get rid of Getrid.

## Letters written in-role

From protesters to local councillors

> Dear Councillor Grey,
>
> We are writing to you to ask about your position on the Getrid bid to buy Moody's old gravel pit in Great Hampton.
>
> We, the undersigned, are

From local councillors to protesters

> Dear Constituents,
>
> I received your letter this morning and found many of your points very interesting. However, having considered the arguments of both sides in this issue, I must

## Village meeting

Set up your space for the meeting. Who is going to chair it? A group member or the teacher in-role? Should he or she be neutral? Try a spontaneous improvisation.

**Gravel Pit Inquiry**

Village Hall 8.00 pm    Saturday Aug. 29th

Getrid representatives and local councillors in attendance.

---

What sorts of questions will be asked at this meeting?
Do the participants need to prepare them?
Does the panel need to think about the sorts of answers they'll give?

> Good evening, ladies and gentlemen. Welcome to this evening's meeting. I can see from the numbers in the audience that this is a . . .

## Hot seating

**Individually – placing quite a lot of pressure on one person – or in groups.**

What do we want to find out?
Information – of a technical or useful nature.
Motivations – why are they behaving like this?
Feelings – guilt? anger? fear? excitement?

**Mr. Moody**

*An individual*

> Don't you have any conscience about ruining the village?

> Yes, I do worry about my village being spoilt but I also think people need jobs.

> I *have* thought about this and consulted my constituents.

> Which constituents? You haven't consulted me!

---

### Getrid manager

*Group of 2, 3 or 4 people representing one person – any one of the group may answer at any time and members of the group can consult each other.*

> Isn't it true that profit is your only motive?

> Certainly not. We are also interested in . . .

### *Anti* local councillor

*Group of 2, 3 or 4 people representing one person – one is the spokesperson while the others sit behind and offer advice.*

## Dealing with the media

### Radio interviews

One or two minutes of airtime.

Working in pairs – one as a reporter, one as a *pro* or *anti* campaigner.

Can you do an interview which gets the point across within the time limit? You could tape it if you wish.

### Whole class

Listen to the interviews.
Which ones got their point across? Why?
Were some more convincing than others?
If so, why?
Which methods were most helpful?

### Newspaper interviews

### Whole group

Look at different styles of journalism:

Tabloid          Quality          Local

Discuss how one set of facts can be reported in very different ways.

How does a reporter get the information required?

*Divide the class into six groups.*

### Three *anti* groups

### Three groups of reporters

Tabloids          Qualities          Locals

*Pair-off the groups.*
*Reporters interview their group and take notes.*
*They might need to formulate some questions before beginning.*

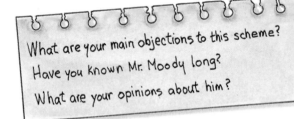

What are your main objections to this scheme?
Have you known Mr. Moody long?
What are your opinions about him?

*Swap groups around.*
*The reporters now become* pro *groups and the* anti *groups become the reporters.*
*Repeat the activity.*

### Reporters

Write your articles and create headlines for them.

Angry mothers are filling the village of Great

### Whole group

### Discussion

Compare the treatment given to the same story by different newspapers.
Are they all telling the truth?
Which gives you the most information?
Does any one of them catch your attention more than the others?

# A TV Programme

*Welcome to* Speak-up *– the programme where you get the chance to sort out problems.*

*Teacher in-role as programme host.*

Each group, in-role, needs to have a meeting to decide the points it wants to bring up and who will raise them.

*I think I should mention potential damage to the church from heavy lorries passing by.*

*Jack, you're unemployed. You should mention the jobs that Getrid will bring.*

## Arguing against strong opposition

### Groups of three

Two *antis*     One *pro*

One *anti*     Two *pros*

### Whole group

Discuss the difficulties experienced. Were any particularly successful strategies discovered?

### Setting up the Speak-up studio

*The show presenter (could be the teacher in-role) opens the programme, gets the argument going and makes sure all sides get a fair crack of the whip.*

## Predicting possible outcomes

In *pro* and *anti* groups, produce still images that suggest what life will be like in the village in five years' time if:
    a) Getrid arrives
or b) the gravel pit is not sold to them.

The still pictures could depict real situations or symbolise the feelings and circumstances of the villagers. Try adding a caption to your still image.

### With Getrid

Working together     v.     Danger all around?
for a better life

### Without Getrid

A healthy place to     v.     Life without work is no
grow up in                        fun

### Discussion

Did the pictures tend to show a bias? Why? Could you also produce an image that shows both the good and bad aspects of each situation?

*We begin this topic by looking at some of the ways in which people deal with each other when problems arise in our society. From this, we move on to the creation of our own new society or community.*

*The children will be examining some or all of the following areas:*

- *How one's own behaviour has a bearing on other's responses*
- *The differences between people – their strengths and weaknesses*
- *The individual's responsibility – both to other individuals and to society as a whole*
- *Leadership – some of the demands it makes on the electorate as well as on the leaders.*

*Schools need to provide 'a balanced and broadly based curriculum that*

**a** *promotes the spiritual, moral, cultural, mental and physical development of pupils at the school and of society; and*
**b** *prepares such pupils for the opportunities, responsibilities and experiences of adult life.'*
*[1988 Education Reform Act]*

*This topic, in addressing matters of personal and social development, makes a useful contribution to such a curriculum.*

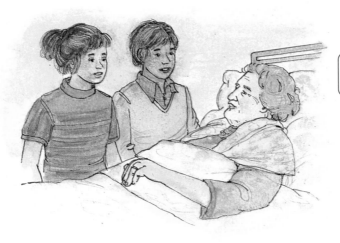

## Class discussion

*Discuss with the class the sort of behaviour we might expect from these three types of people:*

Those who usually put themselves first.

Those who usually put others first.

*Only room for one more.*

*You first luv, I can wait.*

Those who usually balance the needs of others against their own.

*This is where I turn off.*

*Thank you for carrying it so far.*

## Dealing with problems

*Divide the class into these three types. Talk about the difficulties they are likely to experience in trying to represent an opinion other than their own.*

### In groups

*The class is now going to try dealing with some of the problems that can arise in our society.*

*Divide the class into threes, fours or fives, making sure that there is at least one representative of each type in every group. Then give each group a problem to deal with. There are four to start you off on the opposite page.*

*Ask each group to try a spontaneous improvisation in which the people discuss and try to sort out their problem.*

### Whole group

*After the groups have worked for a while, have a discussion of their findings:*

Was there give and take?

Did some people dominate?

Did you weigh the pros and the cons?

Did you reach a solution?

## Problem 1

You are a group of neighbours. In your street there is a very neglected house where an old man lives with his large dog. They are rarely seen. The seeds from his weeds are always blowing into your gardens. The whole place is in an awful state. What do you do?

## Problem 2

You are an adult family group – brothers, sisters, brothers-in-law, sisters-in-law. Your widowed elderly parent is becoming senile and cannot look after him or herself properly. What do you do?

## Problem 3

You are members of the committee that runs your youth club. You have been approached by the organiser of a club for physically and mentally handicapped teenagers. Their premises are being pulled down and they need to find new accommodation. They want to share your building. What do you do?

## Problem 4

You are a group of children. One person in your class is always being bullied by three others. The teachers don't seem to know about it and the person being bullied is too frightened to tell anyone. What do you do?

# A NEW SOCIETY OR COMMUNITY

*Some ideas to consider:*

**What do we mean when we talk about society or community?**

**What would it be like to start a new society or community?**

**When and where might it happen? What shall we choose?**

A new planet?

A desert island?

A space station?

A new housing estate?

A settlement in a new land?

A city where a war has just ended?

Shall we have things like electricity, cars and television or shall we start from scratch?

**In our new society or community, what things shall we encourage and what things shall we forbid?**

Get into pairs and decide.

No violence

No crime

More sports for everyone

We share things

Protection of animals

No swearing

Healthy foods

No animal mess

A clean environment

No child abuse

No drunks

Good education

No bombs

Equal rights

No hooliganism

Employment for all

No drugs

Tidiness

Now pool everyone's ideas.

**Different societies have different needs.
What kinds of people will our society need?**

What will you choose to be?

Carers?

– for animals

– for people

Educators?

Farmers?

Scientists?

Makers?

Builders?

**Thinking about leadership qualities**

If we choose to have some kind of leadership, who would like to try being a leader?

Let's think of things about these people which would make them good leaders. Discuss the qualities that arise. Try to reach a consensus on leadership qualities. *See page 41 on 'Reaching a consensus'.*

Sarah is good at organising
Ali is kind
Maxine has a loud voice!
Fatima stands up for others
David helps people
Leroy is good at explaining

**How will we organise ourselves?**

Do we want
one leader?

Group
leadership?

A voice for all?

**Thinking about a voice for all**

If we choose this way of organising ourselves, how shall we go about it? Does our method truly give a voice to all?

**In pairs**

Think of at least two ways of achieving this:

Open debate.
What happens if some people
do not contribute?

Small discussion groups with a spokesperson for each group. Will there be any problems?

I think . . .

I think . . .

Each person formally asked to give his or her opinion. Will this work?

Shall we have some form of leadership or a voice for all? We need to decide.

## Leadership

Shall we have one leader or a group to lead us? If we choose a group, how many should be in it? Why?

An even number?

We vote no

We vote yes

Or an odd number?

I vote yes

I vote yes

I vote yes

I vote no

I vote no

## Choosing

How are we going to choose our leader/s? Do we want others to know what choice we've made?

I vote for . . .

I vote for . . .

I vote for . . .

Keeping your eyes closed, hands up if your vote is for Venetia.

Do we want to keep it private? What difference does it make?

### Group leadership

If we are choosing a group, how shall we do that?

Venetia X
Ross
Katy X
Fahan
Lee
Yasmin X

Venetia X
Ross
Katy X
Fahan X
Lee
Yasmin

Do we have several votes each or only one?

Venetia X
Ross
Katy
Fahan
Lee
Yasmin

Venetia
Ross
Katy
Fahan X
Lee
Yasmin

What happens if two people get the same number of votes?

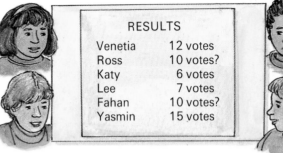

| RESULTS | |
|---|---|
| Venetia | 12 votes |
| Ross | 10 votes? |
| Katy | 6 votes |
| Lee | 7 votes |
| Fahan | 10 votes? |
| Yasmin | 15 votes |

### One leader

If you are electing one leader, does he or she win with a simple majority?

|  |  |  |  |  | Winner ✦ |
|---|---|---|---|---|---|
| Venetia | Ross | Katy | Lee | Fahan | Yasmin |
| 12 | 10 | 6 | 7 | 10 | 15 |
| 45 against | | | | | 15 for ? |

Or do you want to refine your system so that the winner gets an overall majority?

| Venetia | Ross | Katy | Lee | Fahan | Yasmin | |
|---|---|---|---|---|---|---|
| 12 | 10 | 6 | 6 | 7 | 15 | 1st vote Eliminate 2 |
| 19 | 11 | | | 10 | 20 | 2nd Vote Eliminate 2 |
| 33 | | | | | 27 | 3rd Vote |
| ✦ **Winner** – Venetia 33 votes | | | | | | |

Work out a system for our society and then put it into practice.

# A voice for all

## Trying to reach a consensus

*Using the results of the work on 'Leadership qualities' or 'Things we would encourage or forbid in our society', everyone rearranges the items on the list in order of importance, starting with a 1 beside the most important. This must be done secretly.*

Steven

| | |
|---|---|
| No drugs | 8 |
| Good education | 7 |
| Equal rights | 6 |
| No bombs | 2 |
| Healthy food | 3 |
| No violence | 5 |
| Animals protected | 4 |
| No pollution | 1 |

Ali

| | |
|---|---|
| No drugs | 5 |
| Good education | 8 |
| Equal rights | 4 |
| No bombs | 3 |
| Healthy food | 7 |
| No violence | 1 |
| Animals protected | 2 |
| No pollution | 6 |

Natalie

| | |
|---|---|
| No drugs | 8 |
| Good education | 5 |
| Equal rights | 1 |
| No bombs | 2 |
| Healthy food | 4 |
| No violence | 3 |
| Animals protected | 6 |
| No pollution | 7 |

*The lists are then collected and the teacher can add the scores to discover an overall ranking. This needs to be kept secret so that it can be compared with the ranking achieved by consensus.*

## Divide into consensus groups of 4–6 members

You might decide to have mixed groups from your society:

Farmer    Scientist

Builder    Carer

Or you might decide to have specialist groups:

Educationalists    Scientists

Is this likely to make a difference to the results?

## Observers

*One needs to be appointed in each group.*

They are going to:

Watch    and    Listen

They will need a list of all the people in their group.

| | | | | | |
|---|---|---|---|---|---|
| Graham | ✓ | ✓ | ✓ | ✓ | |
| Tina | ✓ | ✓ | ✓ | ✓ | ✓ |
| Ali | ✓ | ✓ | | | |
| Darren | ✓ | ✓ | ✓ | | |
| Katy | ✓ | | | | |

They mark down each time someone speaks, but they don't take part themselves.

The groups now have a set time to reach a consensus on the order of importance of the items on their original lists.

They must not:

appoint a leader

or take votes to decide an issue.

VOTES
KATY ✓
TINA
ALI ✓
DAVID ✓
LEE
YASMIN ✓

*The group must mark the list with the same system of 1 for the most important item and so on. Finally, the whole class considers the experience. Compare the results.*

Was a consensus achieved or not? Why? What behaviour was helpful/unhelpful? Did leaders emerge? *The observers should be able to contribute a great deal to this section.*

## Setting up laws

*This is for groups who chose to have some form of leadership.*

*The leadership needs to draft a body of law.*

*Time can either be given to do this outside the drama session, or the whole class can undertake it in small groups. This may provide a useful background for everyone when questioning of the leaders begins.*

### Leadership presents The Laws

## Finding out about everyone in our new society or community

*The community members introduce themselves and give their occupations. The teacher, in- or out-of-role, can interview or talk to them to find out more and discover what their responsibilities are in our society.*

LAWS
We all share.
There will be no violence.
There will be no cruelty to animals.
There will be no pollution.
There will be employment for all.

### Types of questions that citizens may wish to ask

Do I have to share everything? What happens if I work harder than my neighbour and so have more? Do I have to share it?

When you say 'no violence', does that mean we can't use force to stop someone doing something we think is wrong?

When you say 'no cruelty to animals', does that mean we won't kill them? Will we have to be vegetarians?

I'm Ali, I'm a teacher.

What do you think are the most important things for the children to learn?

I'm Sarah, I'm a doctor.

What are the problems in your job?

I'm Yasmin, I'm a farmer.

What sort of hours do you work, Yasmin?

I'm Peter, I'm a blacksmith.

What else do you make besides horseshoes?

I'm Leroy, I'm a shopkeeper.

Where do all the things you sell come from?

I'm Tina, I make clothes.

Do you have to weave the cloth first?

I'm John, I'm a builder.

Tell us about what you're working on at the moment.

I'm Jane, I'm a scientist.

What is the most important area of your work?

*Having experienced a great deal of verbalisation on this topic, this final section explores some of the physical aspects of it.*

## Creating a work rhythm

### Individually

Find a movement that reflects the meaning of these words.

*Stretch*

*Ooze*

*Squeeze*

*Push*

*Shiver*

*Swirl*

*Wobble*

Try saying the word rhythmically as you repeat the movement. There are lots of words like these. Try some of them. Make your voice sound like the word's meaning.

### In pairs

Imagine a real situation. For example, try to move a large hay-cart that's stuck in the mud.

Use shoulders, back, arms, hands and feet to push and pull. Accompany your work with words and phrases that describe your efforts. For example, heave the cart, pull and strain, push hard, drag. Make sure both your body and voice are working together.

Now choose three or four of your words or phrases and three or four of your movements.
Put them together with your partner and you have a repeatable work rhythm.

Haul the hay

Stuck in the mud

Push and shove

Phew!!

Now, each group – farmers, scientists, etc – see if you can create a work rhythm of movement and words which shows some aspect of your work.

## Creating a living sculpture

### Whole group

This should symbolise our society, its aims and quality of life. Everyone can have a say in its creation if you build it up slowly, starting with two or three people and adding to them.

Think about what you want your tableaux to show.

**Your society's caring nature?**

**Its strength and power?**

**Its emphasis on equality?**

*Although the medieval period falls outside the History Core Study Units for Key stage 2, this topic can be used in several ways:*

- *As part of the following KS2 Supplementary Study Units:*
  *Food and farming*
  *Writing and printing*
  *Domestic life, families and childhood.*

- *Village life input will adapt to KS2 Invaders and settlers (Core Study Unit 1).*

- *It can be used for KS3 Medieval realms (Core Study Unit 2) and Castles and cathedrals (Supplementary Study Unit).*

*There are several opportunities for the teacher to work in-role. Where there are announcements to be made, these could be read, quite legitimately, from a prepared scroll to eliminate any pressure of having to learn by heart.*

*Alternatively, you could improvise at these points if you felt it was appropriate.*

## Becoming a knight

| Choosing a name | Origin |
|---|---|
| Sir John Blynden | (Blond) French |
| Sir Henry Kemp | (A warrior) Old English |
| Sir Percy Powell | (Son of Hywel) Welsh |

## Creating your coat of arms

A coat of arms is always shield-shaped.
You can use only these heraldic colours (tinctures). They should be bold and bright:

### Metals

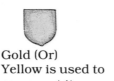

Gold (Or)
Yellow is used to represent it

Silver (Argent)
White is used to represent it

### Colours

Red (Gules) | Blue (Azure) | Black (Sable) | Green (Vert) | Purple (Purpure)

### Furs

Ermine
White with black tails
Gold with black tails
Black with white or gold tails

Vair (squirrel)
Usually blue-white

Some ways of dividing your shield with straight, zig-zag or wavy lines:

Per pale dancy | Quarterly | Per chevron

A bend wavy | A fess wreathy | Lozengy

A saltire engrailed | Bendy sinister

## Charges

(things superimposed on the main background colours)

### Objects

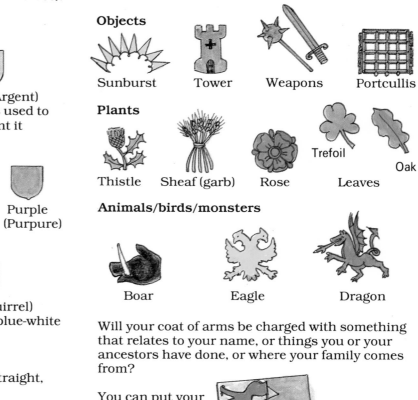

Sunburst | Tower | Weapons | Portcullis

### Plants

Thistle | Sheaf (garb) | Rose | Trefoil | Leaves | Oak

### Animals/birds/monsters

Boar | Eagle | Dragon

Will your coat of arms be charged with something that relates to your name, or things you or your ancestors have done, or where your family comes from?

You can put your coat of arms on a shield made of stiff cardboard.

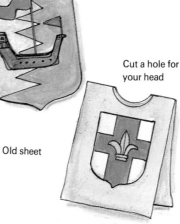

Cut a hole for your head

Old sheet

Or you could make yourself a surcoat or cotte and sew your arms on to it.

## Family stories

### In pairs

When you have made your coats of arms, tell each other stories about your family's history or past.

Some stories might have become exaggerated over the years! Some might be related to things on your coat of arms.

> *My great-great grandfather killed a boar that was so big you wouldn't believe it if I told you! It had been . . .*

> *The ghost of one of my ancestors haunts the battlements every Christmas Eve because . . .*

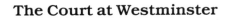

> *Our family came over with William the Conqueror. He granted my ancestor these arms because . . .*

> *Well, the reason we've got three bees on our coat of arms is strange because . . .*

## The Court at Westminster

*In this section, class and teacher work in-role. The children can wear or carry their coats of arms if they have made them.*

Knights, barons and nobles arrive to be greeted by the King's Chancellor Henry Neville (teacher in-role).

> *Welcome, my lords. Will you take a cup of ale?*

> *Did you have a safe journey through the forest?*

> *And how is your wife, the Lady Anne?*

> *My lord, you look truly magnificent. Such a cloth of gold!*

> *A right royal welcome, my lords. Have your steeds been fed and watered?*

> *Ah, my lord, I see you still eat well! We shall feast royally tonight.*

## Oath of allegiance

*You can create your own or you can use the one below.*

Working in-role, the King's Chancellor first calls the meeting to order, then administers the oath and reads the King's message.

*First the oath of allegiance, my lords. Will you raise your right hands.*

*I swear by Almighty God and upon my honour to defend His Majesty the King from all harm and dangers that may beset him.*

My lords,

I am commanded by His Gracious Majesty the King to summon you all here this day in order that he may benefit from your advice on a matter close to his heart.

His Majesty is much troubled by the increasing number of raids and incursions made into his kingdom by the barbarians from the west.

He has therefore decided to build new castles along the western borders to protect his subjects and the land that is rightfully his.

Many of you have built castles on your land – land graciously granted to you by His Majesty – and each one of us has seasoned his sword in many battles and sieges.

Therefore, the King commands that you use your knowledge and experience of these matters to draw up building plans for the strongest fortresses ever seen on this earth.

His Majesty intends holding audience with you when he has dealt with pressing matters of state.

At this meeting you will present your plans to him.

May I suggest you waste no time but set to work immediately.

## Castle plans

### In groups or pairs

Still working in-role, begin to draw up plans. The King's Chancellor can ask questions.

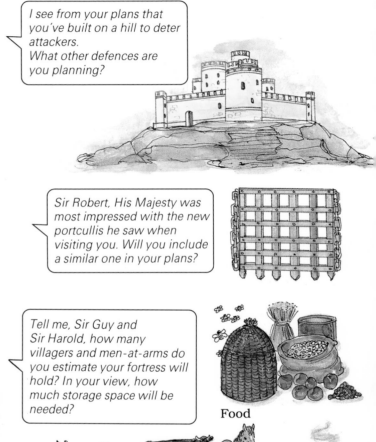

*I see from your plans that you've built on a hill to deter attackers.
What other defences are you planning?*

*Sir Robert, His Majesty was most impressed with the new portcullis he saw when visiting you. Will you include a similar one in your plans?*

*Tell me, Sir Guy and Sir Harold, how many villagers and men-at-arms do you estimate your fortress will hold? In your view, how much storage space will be needed?*

Food

People

Animals

Ammunition

You may need different plans to show different things.

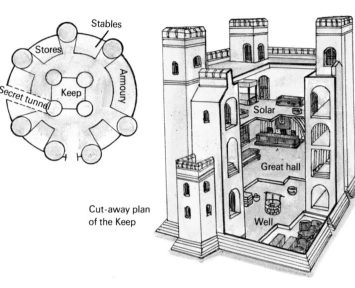

Stables
Stores
Armoury
Keep
Secret tunnel

Cut-away plan of the Keep

Solar
Great hall
Well

### In groups

Practise talking about your plans. If possible, make sure everyone has something to say.

*We think these traps will fool any attacker and . . .*

*On our plans, the defences are – first the outer wall . . .*

*We have made sure there is enough space to store food to last . . .*

How will you carry your plans?

Rolled?

Tied with a ribbon?

Folded?

Unfolded?

Can you manage your shields as well?

### Presentation of plans to the King

*You will need a volunteer to role-play the King as he processes into the meeting. He or she can be given a retinue and the King's Chancellor can be close at hand for support. You could add a fanfare.*

Does everyone signal loyalty as the King passes? How?

By kneeling?

By bowing?

By saluting with shields?

Can you think of other ways?

How can you make sure that each group of knights presents its plans to the King in a way that enables everyone to see?

Which plan will the King choose? Why? Perhaps he will want to take ideas from several plans.

*Time has moved on several years.*
*This next section looks at the lives of villagers living around one of our castles and how they are affected by the threat of attack.*

## LIFE AND WORK IN THE VILLAGE

Try out some of these jobs in mime.

**Where does our food come from? Us!**

Ploughing with oxen – they have to be prodded to keep them going

Harrowing with a metal grid with spikes to prepare for sowing

Sowing corn

Hurling stones with a sling to scare birds

Bee-keeping – honey is our only sweetener and beeswax is used for candles and sealing

Picking fruit

Planting vegetables and weeding

Threshing and winnowing corn

Digging drainage ditches, muck spreading

Milking cows – they provide milk, butter and cheese

**Where do our clothes and the things we use come from? Us!**

How would you wash and shear a sheep?

Handshears

Carding the wool

Spinning        Weaving        Sewing

The potter makes bowls, jugs, pots and storage jars

Blacksmiths have lots of jobs – making and mending things and shoeing horses

Rush lights and tallow dips have to be made to provide light

Furniture has to be made

**Sometimes the whole village needed to work together – for example, haymaking and harvest.**

## A village harvest

Stand in a big circle. Try reaping with large, heavy sickles.

*All equipment such as sickles and haystooks is imaginary.*

Now all swing into the centre together. Can you get a good rhythm?

Try sighing heavily as you swing forward. Change to sighing 'hot', or 'water' or 'cool ale'. Then have a go at saying 'I'm so tired', or 'Oh, my back'. Can you vary the pitch so that some chants are higher and some lower?

Try it like a round (as in singing): for example, a third take 'hot', a third take 'cool ale' and a third 'Oh, my back'. Listen to the sounds and rhythms you make when all working together.

Now form reaping gangs to reap a field. Use the space around you as the field.

As a gang, choose your own chant. In each gang, some will reap and some will gather and make stooks. You may need a different chant for each activity.

As the gangs move across the space together, listen to the sounds and rhythms you make as you work.

> Swing down hard

> Exhausted

Let's move on to stacking the stooks in the barn.

What do you think would be the best way to do this, using everyone here? Choose a method and try it out. Did it work well?

Now you can celebrate after all your hard work with a Harvest Home:

**Feasting and drinking**
Can you make or bring things to eat and drink?

**Games and sports**
One group could create a new game or sport and teach it to the rest.

**Dancing**
You could learn a country dance.

**Singing**
You could learn some lively songs.

*'Sumer is icumen in' can be sung as a round – see the resources section on page 80.*

## An eventful day

*This is a teacher-led creation of a working day. Using the information on these pages or creating your own, narrate the class through part of a village day.*

*You could begin with:*

I'm going to describe the villagers going about their work. We'll need a blacksmith – who'd like to be that? Beekeepers?

*Make sure everyone has a role to play.*

Listen carefully and as soon as you hear what your person is doing, start to join in.

*Before you begin, you could map out the village on the board and relate it to the space you are working in, if you wish.*

It's a warm sunny day in early summer. The villagers are going about their daily work . . .

Besides watching over the pigs rooting around at the edge of the woods, the swineherds are also collecting firewood which is always needed for cooking.

The village potter is busy at the wheel making a large storage jar for Elizabeth, a village woman. Her son dropped her old jar last week. Luckily, it was nearly empty but she needs a new one in time to store food for winter.

In the forge the blacksmith and his son are working over a fierce heat, hammering out horseshoes and sharpening blunted tools. They can feel the sweat dripping down their backs.

In the alehouse Martha, the alewife, is busy brewing beer from barley, water and honey, while also trying to serve two men who are too old to work in the fields but who are still useful. One is carving a spoon and the other is cleaning and sharpening his son-in-law's arrow heads by rubbing them with sand.

Several women have gathered at the well on the green to draw water. There's always a queue, and then there's work waiting to be done at home – a meal to prepare, maybe butter to make or herbs and vegetables to be picked, and there are always clothes to be made or mended.

The blacksmith's wife and daughter are busy peeling rushes and soaking them in fat to make rush lights.

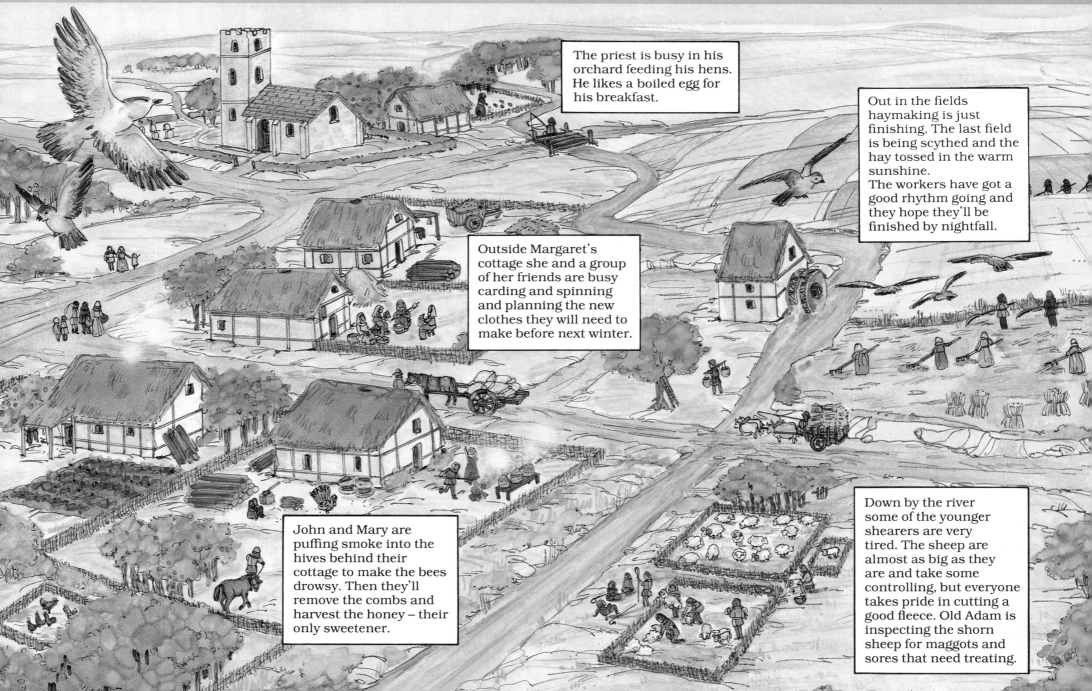

The priest is busy in his orchard feeding his hens. He likes a boiled egg for his breakfast.

Out in the fields haymaking is just finishing. The last field is being scythed and the hay tossed in the warm sunshine.
The workers have got a good rhythm going and they hope they'll be finished by nightfall.

Outside Margaret's cottage she and a group of her friends are busy carding and spinning and planning the new clothes they will need to make before next winter.

John and Mary are puffing smoke into the hives behind their cottage to make the bees drowsy. Then they'll remove the combs and harvest the honey – their only sweetener.

Down by the river some of the younger shearers are very tired. The sheep are almost as big as they are and take some controlling, but everyone takes pride in cutting a good fleece. Old Adam is inspecting the shorn sheep for maggots and sores that need treating.

## Danger approaches

**Either**

*Break into the village work improvisation abruptly by, for example, ringing a bell violently or by rushing in in-role and gathering everyone up.*

**or**

*Take up the narration again. Make up your own or use the following:*

All day they worked. Everyone was tired and hungry and looking forward to the main meal of the day. The smell of baking bread wafted from some cottages to make mouths water.
Suddenly the church bell begins to ring – not the usual steady toll but a wild pealing that strikes fear into everyone's heart.
What is wrong? Dropping their tools they all hurry to the village green.

*Teacher in-role as the lord's messenger*

*People of (name of your village), I have grave news. The rebel Lord Douglas is up to his evil ways again – plundering villages to the north. My Lord Neville has just received a messenger – half dead with exhaustion – who tells us Douglas and his men are half-a-day's march away. They are looting and laying waste everything in their path. My Lord Neville offers you his protection but you, your animals and your possessions must be inside the castle gates by sundown, for then the drawbridge will be taken up for fear of night attack.*
*Take a moment to think what must be done – then hurry!*

### Ideas of things to take

Do the cows, pigs and sheep need herding? Who will do it?

How will we feed them if it's a long siege?

How can we transport all our hens?

What about the bees? Can we take them?

Should we pull up the vegetables in our crofts and take them?

Should we organise moving the haystacks? How will we do it?

Will we need things to protect ourselves?

Rocks and stones? Firewood? Bows and arrows?

What about our tools?

If Douglas' men destroy them, how will we be able to work and grow food again?

*Once the villagers are inside the castle, you could stop the action and ask them to come and look over the battlements in silence.*
*Ask individuals for their thoughts as they look at their abandoned village.*

I wonder if it will look the same tomorrow.

My home looks so small and defenceless.

# Planning, organising, giving orders, negotiating

## Making signalling flags

What could they be used for?

## Groups of five, each including a leader

*Leaders are given instructions and materials away from their group.*

10 sheets of A4 paper

4 rulers

4 pencils

2 pairs of scissors

4 felt tip pens – red, blue, yellow, green

## Leaders' instructions

Your group must produce 10 striped flags:

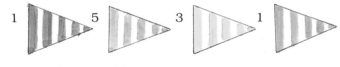

1     5     3     1

red     blue     yellow     green

You must not do the work yourself.

You must try to get the work done quickly and to a high standard.

## Class discussion on completion

Areas to consider:

Leaders   – Did you plan before beginning?

Workers   – Was it easy to understand what you had to do?

Everyone – Did any difficulties arise?
Do you know why?
What would have made it easier?
How did the leader get the group to work?
What effect did his/her way of working have?

## Planning defences

### Whole group

On the board, create a ground plan of your castle.

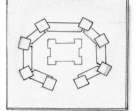

*Divide the class into four, six or eight groups.*

Each group is going to plan the defence of one section of the castle wall. Then, using at least one other group as workers, each group will put its plan into action.

### Things to think about

If there are a lot of casualties, could you still provide adequate defences? How?

What materials will you need? And where will they need to be?

Firewood?     Stones?

Oil and water?     Boulders?     Flaming arrows?

How will you get them in place?

Manpower?     Pulleys?

Can you build any traps?

## Plans into action

### Two organising groups

*Mark out a plan on the floor with chalk or use chairs or forms to define the space. Ensure that both groups have to share some space and materials so that negotiation takes place. For example:*

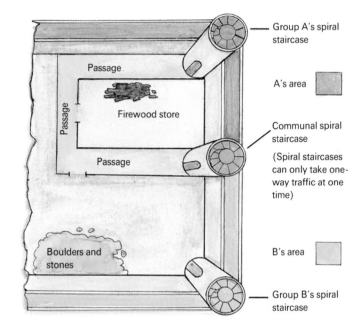

Group A's spiral staircase

Passage

A's area

Communal spiral staircase
(Spiral staircases can only take one-way traffic at one time)

Passage

Passage

Firewood store

Boulders and stones

B's area

Group B's spiral staircase

*Teacher, in-role as Lord Neville, allocates workers to the organising groups who then begin the task.*

### Evaluation

#### Whole group

Did we make the best use of space and time? Which ways of working (strategies) were the most successful? Why? Did the organisers use knowledge gained from the flag-making activity? Did it help? Why?

### Telling stories to keep each other's spirits up

What kinds of stories might you tell each other? Why?

St. George and the dragon?

Travellers' tales?

Courageous actions and deeds?

### In groups

Before beginning the story telling, decide who is going to start his or her story first. With your village friends, find a place and sit down.

Close your eyes and see if you can 'see', in your imagination, the great hall in which you are sitting. The dark stone walls rise up around you. It's very dim and you can't really see into the corners. The whole space is full of people trying not to be too frightened and getting ready to sleep.

Now open your eyes and let the first person start telling his or her story.

### Other ideas

Create a prayer for safe deliverance.

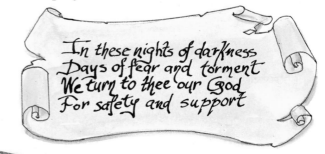

In these nights of darkness
Days of fear and torment
We turn to thee our God
For safety and support

Write Lord Neville's diary entry for the day.

This, the 12th day of June in the year of Our Lord, 1292. This night my castle and lands lie in grave danger. All earthly measures have been taken and we now commit ourselves unto

# The fighting!

*A Do and a Don't*

| **Do** | **Don't** |
|---|---|
| *Always insist on imaginary weapons (no rulers, etc).* | *Miss out the initial introductory steps on control.* |

Certain skills are needed so that no one is hurt.

## Body control

Move around the space, twisting your body into unusual shapes.

Freeze whenever you hear the given signal. Can you hold your position still?

Try it also in slow motion and at double speed.

## Pulling punches

Practise hitting objects but stopping short of touching them.

Now practise being hit by an imaginary hand – in the stomach, in the back and so on.

## In pairs

Make up and number the first six moves of a fight (you must not touch your partner). Try them one at a time with a freeze in between.
If safe, try slow motion and then normal speed.

Do the same exercise with imaginary weapons (swords, axes, flails, etc). Can you keep the imaginary weapons looking the same size and weight?

## In groups

Imagine a small raiding party has scaled the walls and got into the castle. Work out what happens. Remember, no one must touch anyone.

## Finding out about changing feelings

### In groups

Each group creates three tableaux. Imagine they are taken from a tapestry made to record the castle siege – rather like the Bayeux tapestry.

Today, we use 'think' bubbles in comics and magazines to tell the observer what a person is thinking. Use an adaptation of this technique by asking that each person in the tableaux voices one phrase or sentence which tells us his or her thoughts at that time.

**The night before the battle**

*Will I ever see my village again?*

*I'm so frightened*

*I hope I will be brave*

**During the attack**

*This is exciting*

*I'm still frightened*

*I feel powerful*

*I haven't got time to think*

**During the siege**

*This makes me angry. I want to go on fighting*

*Will this ever end?*

*I feel hopeless*

### Whole group

Discuss together the sorts of feelings that were expressed and how they changed throughout the course of events.

## Combating the siege

### Whole group

Lord Neville calls the villagers together in the great hall. Food is running out. What shall we do next?

### First

Carry out a group brainstorm on the problem. Note down every idea.

Messenger pigeons?

Volunteers to create a diversion while others escape under cover of darkness?

Surrender?

Digging a tunnel?

### Second

Evaluate all the ideas and choose the strategies you think you should use.

## Making a radio programme

Imagine that today's radio reporters could be transported back in time. Using a cassette recorder, create a programme that represents a picture of the village, castle and siege.

20th 19th 18th 17th 16th 15th 14th 13th

Things you could include:

### Formal interviews with eyewitness accounts of the battle and siege

*Lord Neville, can I ask you about your tactics?*

*And now we welcome one of the heroines of the siege.*

You will need to give thought to the questions and likely answers.

### Write a ballad or poem about the events

The Ballad of Castle . . .
The night was dark and the cold wind blew
And all the souls on the battlements knew
That when the sun rose . . .

It could be spoken by one voice,

or you could try a choral version,

or you could compose a tune and sing it.

## A roving reporter

He or she could informally 'drop in' on villagers to talk to them as they go about their daily lives.

*And tell me, Margaret, how long does it take you to churn the butter?*

*And may I ask what you're doing?*

*I should have thought that was obvious! It's muck spreading!*

*As I walk over the wooden bridge, I can see the shearers down near the . . .*

Try adding sound effects to lend authenticity to the locations. These could be pre-recorded and (with the use of either a double cassette recorder or two single recorders) played back while recording the interview.

## Create a 'sound picture' of the battle

First, think of all the sounds that an attack on the castle would produce:

Arrows flying

Fires burning

Horses neighing

Shouts, orders, yells, cries!

Oil and water boiling

Clashing of metals

Things falling into the moat

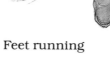

Feet running

Thudding of battering rams

Catapults reverberating

Then experiment with making sounds (be adventurous!). Tape the results and listen to them. You might be surprised.

Some ideas to start you off:

Crackle cellophane, newspaper or polythene in your hand. It can sound like fire.

A rope swung swiftly, or a 'whoosh' with your mouth can sound like arrows flying.

A knife into cabbage can sound like stabbings!

A ruler along a radiator or wicker basket can sound like the ratchets on a catapult.

Metal spoons can sound like fighting.

Finally, add your sounds together and record the result (it will need orchestrating!).

## Working in a match factory in 1888

*This topic lets the class examine life in a match factory at the end of the 19th century. It presents them with a series of events reflecting what happened in 1888. The participants are offered the chance to compare their own feelings and actions with those that took place at the time.*

*You can use one or several of these possible ways in.*

Bring a typical day's meals into the classroom:

Breakfast

Bread        Tea

Dinner

Bread and jam     Cold tea

Supper

Soup      Bread      Tea

Photograph of a group of match factory workers
– taken in London in 1888

Using these two contrasting pictures (this page and the opposite page) and the testimonies (overleaf), discuss the differences you notice.

Try re-creating the pictures in the classroom.

Let the participants voice the imagined thoughts of the people they are representing.
Then have a discussion.

Artist's impression of a match factory in East London – drawn for the *Illustrated London News* in 1871

# TESTIMONY

The living conditions of the Victorian poor and the working conditions of match makers

'The food of these people is totally inadequate . . . consisting largely of a dreary succession of bread, dripping and tea; bread, butter and tea; bacon, bread and coffee; with only a little butcher's meat.'

[Seebohm Rowntree, 1899]

'Lewis Waite's matchworks, Bethnal Green. Consists of 2 small sheds, one a mere lean-to, the other a cart hovel . . . about 20 by 11 feet only, with no ventilation whatever . . . this place serves for both dipping room and drying room, as well as for mixing and heating the sulphur and the phosphorus composition. The smell on entering . . . is quite suffocating, and one would think unendurable for any length of time. A white vapour may be seen constantly rising from the matches. Of course, places for washing, etc. could not be looked for here . . .'

[Mr White's *Report on the Lucifer match manufacturers*, 1863]

'For coverings, the lightest and warmest are the best. Paper is good, very cheap and warm, and it can be burned when it is dirty. Paper blankets are made of two sheets of paper with cotton-wool between. Even a few sheets of newspaper or brown paper pasted together the size of the bed, and put on instead of a top blanket is very much better than nothing. Pillows can be made of . . . torn bits of paper. These are more springy and comfortable if each piece is curled between finger and thumb. It is a nice employment for children and the old folk on winter evenings . . .'

[*A healthy home in one or two rooms*, Edith Barnett, 1881]

'George Gardner, overlooker at Bryant and May's, has known many bad from the work. One lost his jaw. 'You could take his chin (showing) and shove it all into his mouth' . . . has known 18 or 20 lose their jaws . . . has known . . . 11 or 12 who have died from their jaw or their lungs.'

[Mr White's Report, 1863]

'First, the information given does not refer to selected cases. Secondly, there has been absolutely no exaggeration . . . You have to penetrate courts reeking with poisonous and malodorous gases arising from the accumulations of sewage and refuse scattered in all directions. You have to ascend rotten staircases. You have to grope your way along dark and filthy passages swarming with vermin . . . Eight feet square – that is about the average size of very many of these rooms. Walls and ceilings are black with the accretions of filth . . . it is running down the walls; it is everywhere. A window is half stuffed with rags or covered by boards to keep out wind and rain . . . the sickly air which finds its way into the room has to pass over the putrefying carcases of dead cats or birds. As to furniture . . . commonly you will find . . . rough boards resting upon bricks, an old hamper or box turned upside down, or more frequently still, nothing but rubbish and rags.'

[*The bitter cry of outcast London*, Rev. Andrew Mearns, 1883]

'Mr William Bryant of Bryant and May: The mode of manufacture carried on by us is, I believe, perfectly free from any injurious influence upon the health of those engaged in it.'

[Mr White's Report, 1863]

'Halsey's Matchmaking Works, King's Cross. A wretched place, the entrance to which is through a perfectly dark room, much like a cow house. . . . Outside at the back . . . there is a water-butt with a little tub of sickly green water in it. Here, I was told, the children wash. Beyond this . . . is a passage a few feet wide, slightly broader at one end, filled in the middle with a stagnant gutter . . . Here the children eat their meals, unless it be cold or wet, when they eat them round the stove. At the end of this yard, with an open sink or cesspool in front of it, is a single privy common to all . . . and in a very bad state.'

[Mr White's Report, 1863]

'Lewis Waite, employer, can always get workers. Could get a 100 every day if he could employ them. "They come bothering your life out all day pretty near."'

[Mr White's Report, 1863]

## Finding out about factory work

What's the longest time you've kept up the same activity without stopping?
It will probably be a sporting activity.

Skipping?                    Jumping?

Press-ups?

In the 19th century, factory workers had overseers who could beat them if they stopped.

### Whole class

*Ask the class to try doing press-ups with you in-role as the overseer.*

Rules: No talking
No stopping
No slowing down
No laughing

Discuss reactions.

## Thinking about the match making process

How do you think a match was made?

Cutting the wood to size.

Getting the phosphorus on the end.

Phosphorus

Drying off the matches.

Putting the matches in boxes.

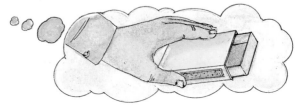

From **The Graphic** on 20th May 1871:

'The "splints" – the wooden bodies of the matches – are brought to the factory in bundles of 2,000.'

Each splint is the length of two matches.

How big do you think a bundle is?

40 makes a bundle about this size.

In a circle, pass round imaginary bundles. Can you make the bundle stay the same size?

## The match making process

*You could ask the class to look at the pictures or you could just talk about the process.*

### Mime

Try these work sequences in mime. What's the best way to do them? How will you work, individually, in pairs or some other way?

### Things to think about

How hot or cold is it?
What is it like in winter and summer?

How easy is it to burn yourself?

Is speed important?
Do you know what piece-work is?

What smells are there?
Hot wax? Charred wood? Phosphorus?

You could reproduce some of these smells.

What sounds are there?
Bubbling wax? Sizzling hotplate?
Roaring or crackling fire?
The sound of the framing machine? Chopping?

Using a cassette recorder, could you make a sound track that would re-create the sounds inside the match factory? You could use it to accompany the mime sequences.

## Charring and waxing to make the wood inflammable

**1.**
Both ends of the splints are charred.

**2.**
The charred ends of the splints are dipped in hot wax.

**3.**
After waxing, the splints are heated again and then left to dry.

## Framing and dipping to add the phosphorus

**4.**
Some splints are stuck together with the wax – rolling loosens them.

**5.**
The machine fits the splints into the frame.

**6.**
The splints are dipped in the phosphorus and left to dry.

## Chopping and boxing the matches

**7.**
The frames are emptied on to the table. If the splints catch alight, the worker is fined.

**8.**
A handful of splints is cut in two.

**9.**
One handful will fill two boxes. A very fast worker could fill 5,184 boxes a day.

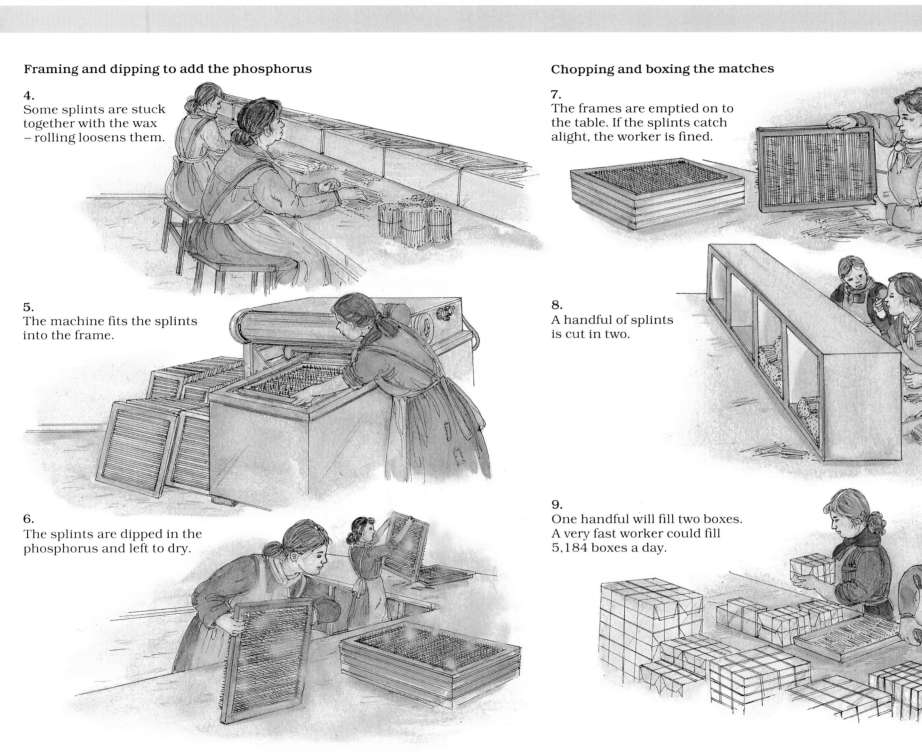

## Being a match worker

### Hours of work

6.30am (summer)/8.00am (winter) to 6.00pm

### Conditions

Many factories were hot, dark and full of suffocating fumes.

## Fines

| | |
|---|---|
| Laughing | 1d |
| Sneezing | 1d |
| Talking | 3d |
| Dirty feet | 3d |
| Litter under bench | 3d |
| Work area dirty | 3d |
| Burnt matches on bench | 1/- |
| Lateness | 5d |

### Rates of pay per week

| From | To |
|---|---|
| 4/- | 9/- |

## Diseases and occupational hazards

'Phossy-jaw' – jaw bone rotted away. This was caused by taking in phosphorus from hands and breathing in fumes.

Baldness – by the age of 15. This was caused by carrying loads on the head.

Burns – from matches catching alight.

Loss of fingers – from dangerous machinery.

## Setting up the factory

If we set up our own
imaginary factory,
who would like to be
the manager?
How would a manager
speak? And behave?

Who would like to be
the overseer?
How would the overseer
behave and speak?
To the manager?
To the workers?
Would the overseer
treat them differently?

### In pairs

Try this out.
What could they be talking about?
How much work has been done?
How well was it done?
Was someone late?

Manager      Overseer

Overseer      Worker

### In groups

The workers were not allowed to speak to each
other but they worked out ways of communicating
which the overseer wouldn't notice.
Could you do that?
Make groups of choppers, dippers or charrers and
see if you can.

Mouthing?      Ventriloquism?      Signing?

### Whole group

Could we turn the space we're in now into our own
imaginary match factory?

If it's the school hall –
do we need to limit
the space we use?

If it's the classroom –
can we use the tables
and cupboards?

Can we use a corner
for the manager's office?

Try out a short sequence from the working day.
Start with a still 'photograph' and then signal with
a click, clap, or word when the photograph comes
to life.

*Let the situation be set up in advance but not
planned, so that the improvisation is
spontaneous and makes lifelike demands.*

## Further ideas to try

### Arriving for work

*You could use the door of the classroom as the factory door.*

Does someone check the workers in?
Is anyone late?
Is it winter or summer?
Have you got shoes?
Have you eaten today?
Do you start to work straightaway?

### Litter left under a bench

What will the foreman or forewoman say?
Do any workers stop to watch?
Will anyone help with the clearing up?

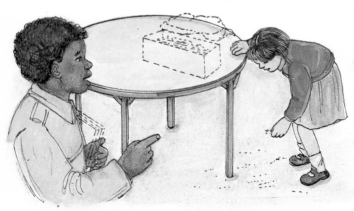

## Collecting pay

Can you sign your name or do you make your mark?
Who pays out the money to the workers?
Has anyone been fined?
Do you think it was fair?

### Giving advice

### In pairs

A younger brother, sister or friend is starting work tomorrow. Tell them the things you think they should know.

## Creating a match worker

*The class can do this individually, in pairs or in groups.*

Draw the outline of your worker. You are going to fill the space inside with information about your person.

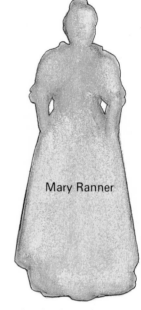

Mary Ranner

Some ideas to think about:

- what is his or her name?
- what does he or she do?
- where does he or she live?
- does he or she have a family?
- is he or she healthy?
- how long has he or she been working?
- is he or she often hungry?
- is he or she quiet or outspoken?
- what does he or she think of the foreman or forewoman?
- does he or she stand up for his or her rights?
- what does he or she think about when working?
- what's the worst or best thing that's ever happened to him or her?
- is he or she often frightened?

Annie Besant (teacher in-role) meets the match workers that the class has created. If a worker has been created by more than one person, any of those involved can answer as the worker – it does not have to be confined to one spokesperson. 'Creators' are also allowed to consult together before answering.

Annie Besant does not have to dress up but if you want to, you could use a shawl or glasses.

*Isn't it you who has a friend with 'phossy-jaw'? How is he or she?*

*Do you have anything to eat before going to work?*

*I can see you have two fingers missing – can you tell me how that happened?*

*Have you ever been fined?*

*Have you ever tried to get things changed?*

*Do you know that fining workers is against the law?*

*What's the worst thing about working in the factory?*

*What are your hours at the factory?*

*How much do you earn?*

*I could report the fines to the factory inspectors because it's against the law. Would you like me to do that?*

After this session the class could write an article, in-role as Annie Besant, exposing the conditions in the Bryant and May match factory. You could take extracts from the original report (overleaf) and compare them with the class's work.

## THE REPORT

'Bryant and May . . . paid last year a dividend of 23 per cent to its shareholders; two years ago it paid a dividend of 25 per cent and the original £5 shares were then quoted for sale at £18 7s. 6d. The highest dividend paid has been 38 per cent.'

'Let us see how the money is made with which these monstrous dividends are paid . . .'

'The hour for commencing work is 6.30a.m. in summer and 8.00a.m. in winter; work concludes at 6.00p.m. Half-an-hour is allowed for breakfast and an hour for dinner. This long day of work is performed by young girls, who have to stand the whole of the time. A typical case is that of a girl of 16, a piece-worker: she earns 4s. a week and lives with a sister, employed by the same firm, who 'earns good money, as much as 8s. or 9s. per week.' Out of the earnings, 2s. is paid for the rent of one room; the child lives on only bread-and-butter and tea, alike for breakfast and dinner, but related with dancing eyes that once a month she went to a meal where 'you get coffee, and bread and butter, and jam, and marmalade, and lots of it.' . . .

The splendid salary of 4s. is subject to deductions in the shape of fines: if the feet are dirty, or the ground under the bench is left untidy, a fine of 3d. is inflicted; for putting 'burnts' (matches that have caught fire during the work) on the bench, 1s. has been forfeited; and one unhappy girl was once fined 2s. 6d. for some unknown crime.

If a girl leaves four or five matches on her bench when she goes for a fresh 'frame', she is fined 3d.; and in some departments a fine of 3d. is inflicted for talking. If a girl is late she is shut out for 'half the day', that is for the morning six hours, and 5d. is deducted out of her day's 8d. One girl was fined 1s. for letting the web twist around a machine in the endeavour to save her fingers from being cut, and was sharply told to take care of the machine, 'never mind your fingers.' Another, who carried out the instructions and lost a finger thereby, was left unsupported while she was helpless.

The wage covers the duty of submitting to an occasional blow from a foreman; one, who appears to be a gentleman of variable temper, 'clouts' them 'when he is mad.'

One department of the work consists in taking matches out of a frame and putting them into boxes; about three frames can be done in an hour, and $\frac{1}{2}$d. is paid for each frame emptied; only one frame is given out at a time, and the girls have to run downstairs and upstairs each time to fetch the frame, thus much increasing their fatigue. One of the delights of the frame work is the accidental firing of the matches; when this happens the worker loses the work, and if the frame is injured she is fined or 'sacked'. 5s. a week had been earned at this by one girl I talked to.

The 'fillers' get $\frac{3}{4}$d. a gross for filling boxes; at 'boxing' i.e. wrapping papers round the boxes, they can earn from 4s. 6d. to 5s. a week. A very rapid 'filler' has been known to earn once 'as much as 9s.' in a week, and 6s. a week 'sometimes'.

The making of boxes is not done in the factory; for these 2$\frac{1}{4}$d. a gross is paid to people who work in their own homes, and 'find your own paste'. Day-work is a little better paid than piece-work, and is done chiefly by married women, who earn as much sometimes as 10s. a week, the piece-work falling to the girls . . .

A very bitter memory survives in the factory. Mr Theodore Bryant, to show his admiration of Mr Gladstone and the greatness of his own public spirit, bethought him to erect a statue to that eminent statesman. In order that his workgirls might have the privilege of contributing, he stopped 1s. each out of their wages, and further deprived them of half-a-day's work by closing the factory, 'giving them a holiday'. ('We don't want no holidays', said one of the girls pathetically, for – needless to say – the poorer employees of such a firm lose their wages when a holiday is 'given'.)

So furious were the girls at this cruel plundering, that many went to the unveiling of the statue with stones and bricks in their pockets, and I was conscious of a wish that some of those bricks had made an impression on Mr Bryant's conscience. Later on they surrounded the statue – 'We paid for it' they cried savagely – shouting and yelling, and a gruesome story is told that some cut their arms and let their blood trickle on the marble paid for, in very truth, by their blood.

Such is a bald account of one form of white slavery as it exists in London . . . Who cares for these white wage slaves? Born in slums, driven to work while still children, undersized because underfed, oppressed because helpless, flung aside as soon as worked out, who cares if they die or go on the streets, provided only that the Bryant and May shareholders get their 23 per cent . . . Oh, if we had but a people's Dante, to make a special circle in the Inferno for those who live on this misery, and suck wealth out of the starvation of helpless girls.

Failing a poet to hold up their conduct to the execration of posterity, enshrined in deathless verse, let us strive to touch their consciences, i.e. their pockets, and let us at least avoid being 'partakers of their sins', by abstaining from using their commodities.'

[White slavery in London, *Link Magazine*, June 1888]

## What might happen at the factory after the article is published?

Try out a meeting between the manager and the foreman or forewoman.

You can use 'forum theatre' so that you can stop at intervals to discuss what has happened and let different people attempt to deal with the situation.

*Have you read this?*

*Sorry, not very good at reading, Sir.*

*Find me the ringleaders.*

*I know who'll talk if I drop them a shilling.*

*These workers are getting too big for their boots.*

*Just leave it to me Sir, I'll knock it out of them.*

Try one or more of your ideas with the rest of the class as the workers.

In the 1888 Match Strike the workers were asked to sign documents stating that they were well treated.

Set up your factory again and call the workers in to sign a document. Will they?

*You can photocopy the one below.*

Bryant & May

I ..............................
hereby swear that during my employment at Bryant and May I have been well treated, and that I am satisfied with my position.

Signed ...............................

2nd July 1888

Perhaps they will all sign or make their mark.

Perhaps some will refuse.

Perhaps some will get sacked.

Perhaps some will strike.

Discuss the reactions and compare them with those of 1888.

'To be torn up from the roots of home life and to be sent away from the family circle, in most instances for the first time in the child's life, was a painful event . . . From the first day of September 1939, evacuation ceased to be a problem of administrative planning. It became instead a multitude of problems in human relationships.'

[Richard M. Titmuss]

*This topic offers opportunities to consider the evacuation from both sides – as evacuees and as the host families who received them.*

## What is an evacuee?

### Group discussion

Just a line or two from me,
A happy little evacuee
It comes to bring my love and say
Good luck be yours from day to day

Thought I'd drop a line.

A postcard from the period

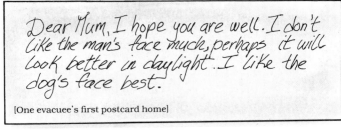

Dear Mum, I hope you are well. I don't like the man's face much, perhaps it will look better in daylight. I like the dog's face best.

[One evacuee's first postcard home]

## Thinking about separation

### Group discussion

Have you ever stayed away from home without your parents?

At Cub or Brownie camp?

Familiar bedtime routines?

In hospital?  With a friend or relations?

*O sole mio, give it to me*

Familiar sounds?

Your usual food?

What did you miss?

Your pet?

Getting a cuddle?  Your toys?

### In pairs

Imagine that you and your partner are evacuees today. Tell each other the two things you miss most and see if you can describe how you feel without them. Then take it in turns to tell the whole class how your partner feels.

## Looking at the problems facing three groups

*Divide the class into three groups representing children, parents and teachers. Let each group spend some time deciding what would be its thoughts, feelings and actions in the run up to evacuation day.*

### Hot-seating each group

Some questions to start you off:

What's worrying you most?

What have you been doing to prepare for evacuation?

Have you spoken to your parents/child/children about what's happening?

A poster from the period

### Children

### Parents

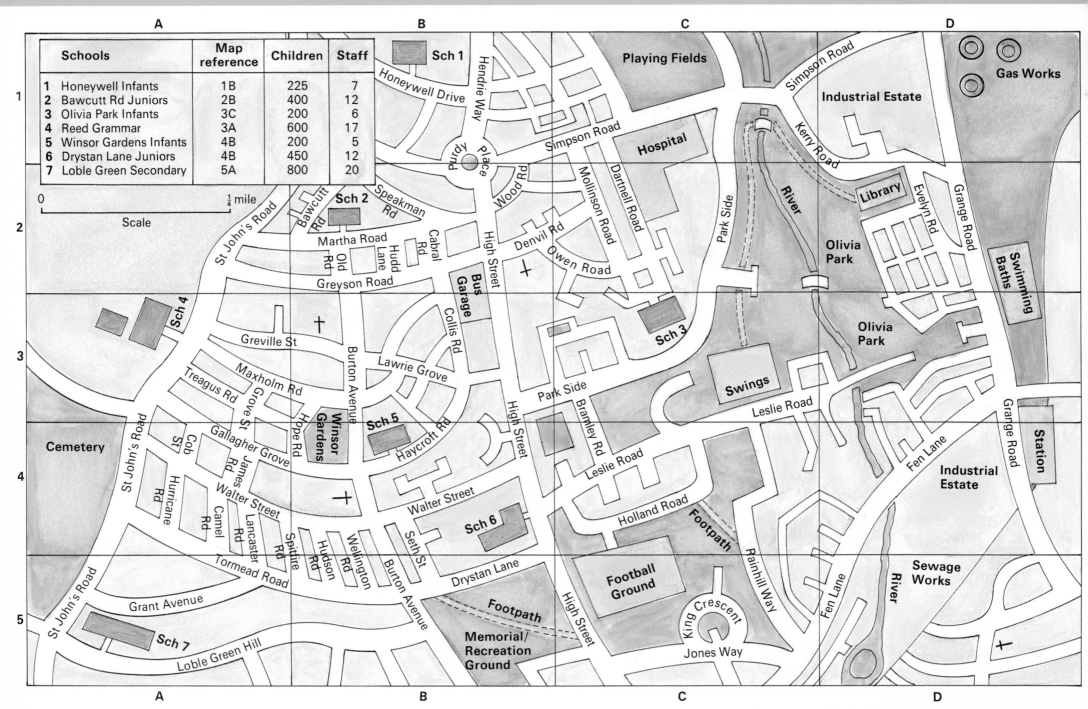

| Schools | | Map reference | Children | Staff |
|---|---|---|---|---|
| 1 | Honeywell Infants | 1B | 225 | 7 |
| 2 | Bawcutt Rd Juniors | 2B | 400 | 12 |
| 3 | Olivia Park Infants | 3C | 200 | 6 |
| 4 | Reed Grammar | 3A | 600 | 17 |
| 5 | Winsor Gardens Infants | 4B | 200 | 5 |
| 6 | Drystan Lane Juniors | 4B | 450 | 12 |
| 7 | Loble Green Secondary | 5A | 800 | 20 |

0 — ¼ mile

Scale

## Getting to the station

*Divide the class into seven groups representing the staff from each school.*

**Brief:**

**All staff and children must be at the station by 10.30am.**

1. Which route will you take? Why?
   Are there likely to be any problems?

2. How will you organise the children?
   Will they be in one big group? Or broken up into smaller ones?

3. Do you need to consult with other schools in your area? If you feel it would be useful, then do so.

4. Will the weather make any difference to your plans?

5. How long do you estimate it will take?
   What time will you leave?

*Each group can prepare a written or oral report for the District Evacuation Officer (teacher in-role). The report can then be used for an in-role evaluation of the experience:*

Have arrangements been made to cope with seven schools arriving at the station at the same time?

Has thought been given to the problem of more than one school using the same route?

Did schools consult each other successfully?

Have different walking speeds been taken into account?

How successful are our plans likely to be?

*Other ideas:*

## Crossing the road

### In groups, in-role as teachers

Can you think of a quick and safe method of getting large groups of children over main roads without causing major traffic hold-ups?

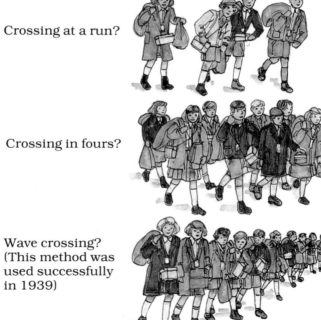

Several classes at once?

Crossing at a run?

Crossing in fours?

Wave crossing? (This method was used successfully in 1939)

Set up a 'road' in the school hall or playground. Try out your methods, assessing them for safety and speed.

## Learning songs the children sang

'Ten Green Bottles'          'Run Rabbit Run'

'Underneath the Spreading          Chest          Nut          Tree'

## Making things you will need

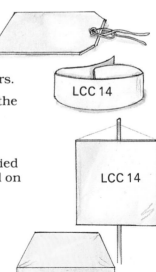

Brown paper labels.

Arm-bands for the teachers.

These were marked with the school's number.

The banner that was carried at the head of each school on the march to the station.

A box to carry your gas mask in. What will you make it from?

How will you carry it?
How strong should it be?
What's the best shape?

## The day before evacuation

### Whole group

*Set up a 1939 classroom with chairs in rows (the desks can be imagined) and four or five children as teachers. Each 'teacher' can take a row of children as his or her class.*

*Teacher in-role as WVS (Women's Voluntary Service) worker:*

> *Good morning, children. I am from the WVS and I'm here to tell you that the evacuation will take place tomorrow. Although war has not yet been declared, our government thinks it best to have a safe and orderly evacuation now to make sure you are not placed in any unnecessary danger. So please go with your teachers who will remind you of everything you need to bring tomorrow. Remember – no drinks, in case bottles get broken, and no pets under any circumstances.*

*In class groups, 'teachers' deal with any queries and remind children of what they need to bring.*

Evacuation Checklist

CLASS 2

Clothing
Washing things
Personal belongings
*All in one bag or parcel*

Packed lunch
Fruit
*No drinks*
Gas mask and case

### Class discussion

How will the children be feeling? What might they do on their last night at home?

## Special objects

### Whole group

Imagine you are sorting out your things to be packed. Choose one thing to take with you that you really value. Pick it up carefully and gather round.

Let each person talk about his or her object:

> *This is a photo of my mum to remind me of her every day. I don't want to forget what she looks like.*

> *I've had my teddy since I was two. I always take him to bed.*

> *This is my dog's old collar. I shall miss him very much, his coat is very soft.*

> *This locket was given to me by my grandma. She and my grandad look after me a lot of the time and I'll miss them.*

> *This book is my favourite, it makes me laugh and my dad reads it to me.*

> *I got this model car for my last birthday. It's my favourite.*

### Possible points for class discussion

How do our special objects help us? Do they cheer us up? Remind us of happy times? Give us comfort? Which special object would we want to keep with us today? Have you ever lost something very precious to you? How did you feel?

## Evacuation Day

*Teacher in-role as the Head Teacher or WVS worker.*

### Teachers and classes

Taking the register.

| | | | |
|---|---|---|---|
| | | | LCC 14 |
| Sarah Abel | ✓ | ✓ | ✓ |
| Ann Best | ✓ | ✓ | ✓ |
| Linda Cray | 0 | ✓ | ✓ |
| Ann Cray | ✓ | ✓ | ✓ |
| Enid Rider | ✓ | 0 | ✓ |

Getting labels written and tied on.

Drystan Lane Juniors
LCC 14

Linda Cray
2 Orchard Terrace
East Ham
London

LCC 14

Putting arm-bands on teachers.

Getting classes lined up with the banner at the front.

LCC 13

The classes can now march to the station – singing on the way.

*Run rabbit, run rabbit, run run run; run rabbit, run rabbit, run run run;*

*Bang, bang, bang, bang, goes the farmer's gun, run rabbit, run rabbit, run run run;*

*Run rabbit, run rabbit, run run run, don't give the farmer his fun fun fun;*

*He'll get by without his rabbit pie, so run rabbit, run rabbit, run run run.*

LCC 15

LCC 14

*You can limit this activity to the classroom or you could expand into the school hall or even into the playground!*

Make train carriages from chairs or benches (there were often no corridors on trains of this period).

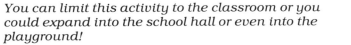

Try creating two photographs – one at the start of the journey and the other at the end of a trip which could have been six or eight hours' long.

## Village host families

### Who might they be?

Farmers

Shopkeepers

Blacksmith

Baker

Vicar

Policeman

Doctor

Teacher

Housewives and mothers

## First village meeting

*Teacher in-role as Billeting Officer.*
*Arrange space and chairs as in a village hall.*
*Explore the situation by encouraging questions*
*from villagers.*

Thank you all for responding so splendidly and coming along at such short notice this afternoon. We all lead very busy lives and can ill afford the time. But, as you know, we have been chosen as a host area for evacuees and I have just received notice that we are to expect the arrival of up to 100 children tomorrow. It is vital that everyone plays his or her part, but I feel sure we will all open our homes to these children in their hour of need. The government has promised a sum of 10s. 6d. for the first child and 8s. 6d. per week for every other child you take. Now before we all go off to prepare, are there any questions?

What time will they arrive?

What happens if they are ill?

Where will they go to school?

What time should they go to bed?

Will they know how to behave in the country?

How old are they?

Where are the children coming from?

The meeting could draw up a set of guidelines for both hosts and evacuees and/or a plan of the village.

## Preparing for the evacuees

### Thought-tracking and mime

### In pairs

One partner speaks the person's thoughts while the other mimes the person's actions.

*I'll keep all my best china locked up. I've heard that some of these children are very rough!*

*Bedtime will probably be difficult. They'll get upset then.*

*What I want is a couple of good strong boys. They'd be very useful on the farm – as long as they behaved themselves.*

Watch some or all of the pairs and discuss the villagers' thoughts. Are they realistic?

## Arrival of the evacuees

### Testimony

'When we arrived inside the school room I thought of . . . (an) ancient slave market. The villagers were whispering to each other, "Shall we have this one?" or "That one over there looks fairly clean."'

[Teacher]

'Some children treated it as a great adventure, others sat silently, scarcely able to take in the scene, others quietly sobbed as they were handed over to foster mothers.'

[Cub aged 10, Cheshire]

'I was just six years old when my mother hung this label round my neck and sent me off to be an evacuee . . . In the very first place I stopped at, the son of the household looked me up and down and then deliberately spat in my face.'

[Tom Bell, actor]

'It was like a slave market – one man came saying, "The missus has just had a new baby, we'll have a good strong girl to help her."'

[Scholarship girl]

'The woman said, "I don't want *her* – she's too ugly." That was me. I cried. The voluntary worker said, "Well look, let your brother and sisters go with this lady, and you go with this other one."'

[Joyce, Spitalfields]

Evacuees arriving at their billet in 1939

'She told him . . . if he wanted her he must take me too. He went home to ask his wife if she could have two children. She agreed, so he returned to collect us. When he arrived I started to cry and refused to go. The old man went to the nearest florist and bought an enormous bunch of flowers for me.'

[Girl aged 4, Liverpool]

'For the most part the children were too tired and bewildered to cry.'

[*War in the countryside*, Sadie Ward]

## The handing over

### Whole group

Prepare role-cards for a small group of villagers.

You look upon this as a new challenge and you like a challenge.

You feel rather frightened of the rough city children you've heard about.

You dislike the idea of a child in your home. You want one who won't be in the way.

You want a strong worker to help on your farm.

You feel sorry for the children – you know how upset your own children would be if they had to leave home.

You just want a child to love. You haven't got any of your own.

## Still image and spontaneous improvisation

*The group representing the villagers can use the rest of the class to build a 'photograph' of the children who are waiting in the village hall.*

Hold the picture still for a moment. You could ask for a word or phrase that sums up what each person feels. Let the still photo come to life with the arrival of the villagers to choose a child. Will all the children be chosen? What does it feel like to be the last one or to be left over? Discuss.

## Voicing thoughts

### Individually

Imagine unpacking your things in your new bedroom. Whisper aloud to yourself what you are thinking and feeling as you put things away.

Does seeing your darned socks remind you of mum? 'I wish she was here. I'd feel all right then.'

Does the photograph of you, your mum, dad, grandma, brothers and sisters just make you whisper 'I want to go home'?

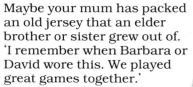

Maybe your mum has packed an old jersey that an elder brother or sister grew out of. 'I remember when Barbara or David wore this. We played great games together.'

## Writing the first postcard home

You could make the postcard first, drawing a picture for the front or leaving it plain.

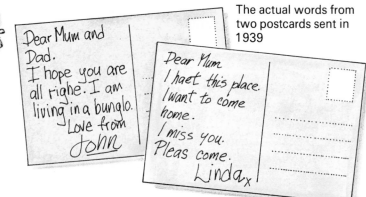

The actual words from two postcards sent in 1939

Dear Mum and Dad.
I hope you are all righe. I am living in a bunglo.
Love from John

Dear Mum
I haet this place. I want to come home.
I miss you. Pleas come.
Linda x

### Whole class

Read some of the cards. Do they give a true picture of how the writer feels? What do you think the mums and dads will feel when they read them?

## Testimony

> 'The children were only accustomed to obey when cuffed or shouted at – this was true of at least 50 per cent.'
>
> [From *War in the countryside*]

> 'The (village) teacher . . . kept saying, "Sharp as pins you are, bright as buttons you are." She was ever so pleased that the war had come because it meant she had got some bright children.'
>
> [From *Don't you know there's a war on?*]

> '"Cor, I don't 'alf feel funny" – an evacuee from East London after being forcibly bathed.'
>
> [From *Who will take our children?*]

> 'Poverty of appearance and manners, late nights, head lice, rough street games, smoking, swearing, chips with everything, bedwetting, some or all of which were common to children from the poorest areas in London, provoked a storm of outrage within the receiving communities.'
>
> [From *London at war*]

## Second village meeting

### Whole group with teacher in-role

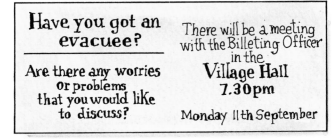

**Have you got an evacuee?**

Are there any worries or problems that you would like to discuss?

There will be a meeting with the Billeting Officer in the **Village Hall** **7.30pm**

Monday 11th September

## Some possible problems

- If a child is lost, how can we find out where he or she belongs?

- Can we get any help with children who wet the bed? Washing costs money.

- What do we do if a child's parents or relatives are killed? Do we tell them?

- How can we help the evacuees and local children to get on together?

- If a child is ill, should we let the parents know?

*If the teacher works as the Billeting Officer, he or she is in a good position to feed in information. Alternatively, a briefed child or group could take this on if you would prefer to be a villager.*

## Dealing with problems

### Small groups

#### Prepared improvisations

Each group takes a problem that has arisen in the village. The improvisations need to explore how the villagers deal with these problems.

Children smoking in the hay barn

Teasing animals

Gates being left open

## Whole group

### Forum theatre

Watch the prepared improvisations and discuss the methods of dealing with the problems. Then allow the watchers to try out different ways.

## Letter to a relation

2 The Lane
Ditcham
3. 10. 39

Dear Edith,
It's now a month since our evacuees arrived. They seem to be settling down quite well now, though

## Diary entries as a villager or a child

Sept 4. – Went to bed exhausted. My evacuees are proving quite a handful. I found the boy chasing the chickens through the orchard and he was really quite rude when I corrected him. Oh dear, I hope we shall be able to cope.

Sept 8. – Four days since I last wrote. I've been so busy – the children arrived with hardly any clothes.

## General books

Bolton, G., *Drama as Education*, Longman, 1984

Davies, G., *Practical Primary Drama*, Heinemann Educational, 1983

HMI, *Curriculum Matters 17: Drama from 5 to 16*, HMSO, 1989

Linnell, R., *Approaching Classroom Drama*, Edward Arnold, 1982

Neelands, J., *Making Sense of Drama*, Heinemann, 1984

O'Neill, C., et al., *Drama Guidelines*, Heinemann, 1976

Rawlins, G. and Rich, J., *Look, Listen and Trust*, Macmillan Educational, 1985

## Resources for topics in this book

### ORAL FLUENCY

Most of these books are intended for ESL teachers but they contain many ideas that can be used for oral language work in the primary classroom.

Maley, A. and Duff, A., *Drama Techniques in Language Learning*, Cambridge University Press, 1978

Milroy, E., *Role Play* (chapter on conversational skills), Aberdeen University Press, 1982

Nolasco, R. and Arthur, L., *Conversation*, 1987

Porter Ladousse, G., *Role Play*, 1987

Wessels, C., *Drama*, 1987

(The above three titles are in the series 'Resource Books for Teachers', ed. Alan Maley, Oxford University Press, 1987.)

### FAMINE

Band Aid, *School Aid Pack*

### CHEMICAL DUMP

Seymour, J. and Girardet, H., *Blueprint for a Green Planet*, Dorling Kindersley, 1987

### CASTLES AND VILLAGE LIFE

Hartley, D., *Food in England*, Macdonald, 1954

Hartley, D., *The Land of England*, Macdonald, 1979 (This book is full of information about country life through the ages.)

Macdonald, F., and Bergin, M., *Inside Story: A Medieval Castle*, Simon & Schuster Young Books, 1990

Oliver, S., *An Introduction to Heraldry*, Apple Press, 1987

Puttock, Colonel A. G., *A Dictionary of Heraldry and Related Subjects*, Blaketon Hall Ltd, 1985

Wise, Hook and Walker, *Medieval Heraldry* ('Men-at-Arms' series), Osprey Publishing, 1980

#### Music and dance

EMI Records, *Spectacular Sound Effects: Album 2, Fanfares*, THIS 35 record or cassette

Lobley, P. and Lobley, R., *Your Book of English Country Dancing*, Faber and Faber, 1980

Stuart, F., *Stories of Britain in Song* ('Sumer is icumen in'), Longman Young Books, 1972

Books, records and tapes can be obtained from:

The English Folk Dance and Song Society
Cecil Sharp House
2 Regent's Park Road
London NW1 7AY
(Tel: 071 485 2206)

### MATCHGIRLS

Adams, C., *Ordinary Lives – A Hundred Years Ago* Virago, 1982

Rawcliffe, M., *Finding Out about Victorian Towns*, Batsford Educational, 1982

Royston Pike, E., *Human Documents of the Industrial Revolution in Britain*, Allen and Unwin, 1966

Royston Pike, E., *Human Documents of the Victorian Golden Age*, Allen and Unwin, 1967

Then and There Film Strips, *Victorian Social Life – Some Things Victorian People Said and Wrote* (Booklet), Longman/Common Ground, 1979

Thornton, E., *Brick Lane – A Historical Study of Settlement*, ILEA, 1983

A few photographs of matchgirls and matchbox makers are held at:

The Labour History Museum
103 Princes Street
Manchester MI 6DD
(Tel: 061 228 7212)

The museum also sells a pamphlet, *The Matchgirls' Strike 1888*, by Reg Beer.

### EVACUEES

#### Non-fiction
Croall, J., *Don't You Know There's a War On?*, Hutchinson, 1988

Haining, P., *The Day War Broke Out*, W. H. Allen, 1989

Jackson, C., *Who Will Take Our Children?*, Methuen, 1985

Lewis, P., *A People's War*, Methuen, 1986

Longman, N., *How We Lived Then*, Hutchinson, 1971; Arrow, 1973

Mack, J. and Humphries, S., *London at War*, Sidgwick and Jackson, 1985

Massey, V., *One Child's War*, Ariel, 1978

Ward, S., *War in the Countryside*, Cameron, 1988

Westall, R., *Children of the Blitz*, Viking, 1985

*Where's Your Horns?*, Spitalfields, 1979

#### Fiction
Magorian, M., *Goodnight Mr Tom*, Kestrel, 1981

#### Music
Gay, N. and Butler, R., *'Run, Rabbit, – Run!'*, Noel Gay Music Co. Ltd., 1939